AMERICA'S FEMME FATALE

Brynhild Paulsdatter Storset, later to be known as Bella Sorenson and then Belle Gunness. *Photo courtesy of La Porte County Historical Society.*

AMERICA's FEMME FATALE

The Story of Serial Killer
BELLE GUNNESS

JANE SIMON AMMESON

RED ⚡ LIGHTNING BOOKS

This book is a publication of

Red Lightning Books
1320 East 10th Street
Bloomington, Indiana 47405 USA

redlightningbooks.com

Manufactured in the United States of America

First printing 2021

Library of Congress Cataloging-in-Publication Data

Names: Ammeson, Jane, author.
Title: America's femme fatale : the story of serial killer Belle Gunness /
   Jane Simon Ammeson.
Description: Bloomington, Indiana : Red Lightning Books, [2021] | Includes
   bibliographical references.
Identifiers: LCCN 2021013229 (print) | LCCN 2021013230 (ebook) | ISBN
   9781684351596 (paperback) | ISBN 9781684351619 (ebook)
Subjects: LCSH: Gunness, Belle, 1859–1908. | Serial
   murderers—Indiana—LaPorte County—Biography. | Women serial
   murderers—Indiana—LaPorte County—Biography.
Classification: LCC HV6517 .A46 2021 (print) | LCC HV6517 (ebook) | DDC
   364.152/32092 [B]—dc23
LC record available at https://lccn.loc.gov/2021013229
LC ebook record available at https://lccn.loc.gov/2021013230

To my parents, Dan and Lorraine Simon,
who loved a good mystery,
and to my husband, John Fields,
who is always there for me.

CONTENTS

PREFACE

WHEN ASHLEY RUNYON, THEN MY EDITOR AT INDIANA UNIversity Press, first asked me to write a book about Belle Gunness, I wondered what was new to write about. After all, from the very first day of discovery, the story of Belle's murder farm garnered national attention. A deluge of reporters, including some from New York, San Francisco, Los Angeles, and Washington, descended upon La Porte, Indiana, a charming and prosperous city circling the shoreline of a large inland lake with tree-lined boulevards of stately homes and a Victorian-era downtown.

The sensational discovery of the butchered body of Andrew Helgelien, a Norwegian farmer who, after visiting Belle in LaPorte, cashed out all his savings and then disappeared, setting his brother Asle on a mission to find him, spurred further searches of the property. They discovered an amazing tangle of rotted body parts and skeletal remains of men, women, and children.

The finding sent reporters and police on a quest to explore every aspect of Belle Gunness's life. Almost every day a new fact was uncovered. It made for thrilling reading, and reporters, some of whom spent weeks in La Porte, were filing one-hundred-thousand-word stories to meet the demand.

Just when it couldn't get more bizarre, it always did.

The murder farm became a carnival scene with gawkers arriving on special trains packed to capacity and grieving relatives searching among the decaying remains hoping to find their loved ones in the makeshift morgue. But Belle had been prodigious in her use of quicklime, and little was left to be identified, just oozing, putrid masses of flesh and bones.

The news ratcheted up with reports of midwifery and abortions performed late at night, matrimonial agencies sending victims to her house, and connections between Belle and another mass murderer, now mostly forgotten, Johann Hoch. The number of people Belle murdered is difficult to assess. Sheriff Albert Smutzer called off the digging even though there were still soft spots in the earth indicative of burials and many, many families still desperate to find their loved ones. Most likely there are still victims beneath the earth on the farm today.

An odd assortment of players populated Belle's story, including Elizabeth Smith, a once-beautiful woman who kept a skull in her home for séances and was called a voodoo queen, and Julius Truelson, a man in jail for forged checks in Texas who confessed to helping Belle dispose of bodies in exchange for her agreement to do away with his first wife. Belle's ex-handyman and lover, Ray Lamphere, alcoholic and consumptive, told lots of stories about what happened that fateful night when Belle's secrets came to light.

Though there's no lack of "information," much of what has been written is wrong—back then, a lack of reliable communication led to errors as did suppositions and stories told by those with their own agendas. But even now, facts I've taken from the coroner's inquest—typed up from handwritten notes by forensic anthropologist Andrea Simmons, transcribed from contemporary witnesses and thus accurate—are misrepresented in newspaper and magazine articles, not to mention on websites. Even reading the same story in two or more different papers of the time isn't verification. Sometimes a story would go out on the wire with errors, and it would suddenly spread throughout the country. Large papers in big cities that could send their reporters to La Porte and local papers near where the crimes occurred often excelled in their coverage. Others less so.

Researching this book, I also relied on historians and scientists who tend not to make speculative judgments. I cross-referenced newspaper sources and read interviews with those still alive when such books as *The Truth About Belle Gunness* by Lillian de la Torre, a noted crime writer so famous and respected that her obituary appeared in the *New York Times*, were researched and written.

For more about the missing men and women, I read the papers from the towns where they lived as they often did extensive stories including interviews with the grieving families and contacted the local libraries and historical societies to dig for more information.

While this story is written as narrative nonfiction, any material within quotation marks or set as an excerpt has been verified as the exact words spoken or reported.

Belle liked to write letters; it was how she lured men to her farm. I've read the letters still in existence that were translated from Norwegian, provided to me by journalist Ted Hartzell, who came into their possession years ago. Belle had a cruel and arrogant sense of humor. According to Katherine Ramsland, professor at DeSales University in Pennsylvania who has written extensively about serial killers and has studied the letters, when Belle refers to "smooth and evil people" who are up to "fraud and tricks" in one of her letters to Andrew, "she must have taken such delight in saying that, knowing what she herself was up to. Again, this is classic sociopathic behavior. People like Belle enjoy their own ingenuity and deception; the joke is on the victim who deserved it for being such a dupe. She even has a little joke, funny only to her, writing how he might work himself to 'death' if he stays here."

Here's another sick joke she's said to have played. Her hogs were prized for their taste though it must have turned quite a few stomachs when Ray Lamphere revealed that she sometimes diced up body parts and put them out into the pig lot. And her sausages might not have been wholly made out of pork. Imagine her sly, superior smile when people complimented her on the taste of her pork chops and sausage. The joke, again, was on them. They were stupid; she was smart. She was Belle Gunness, all powerful and impossible to defeat—and she was for a long time. But maybe not forever.

Belle, if all the stories are true, meets the criteria, according the *Diagnostic and Statistical Manual of Mental Disorders*, fifth edition, for someone who has an antisocial personality disorder (ASPD). People with this disorder are incapable of understanding others' feelings; often use mind games or manipulation to control friends, family members, coworkers, and even strangers; show a lack of regard for others' feelings; and are capable of violating the rights of others. Other characteristics of ASPD that fit with what we know of Belle include: doesn't respect social norms or laws, consistently breaks laws or oversteps social boundaries, lies, deceives others, uses false identities or nicknames, uses others for personal gain, and doesn't feel guilt or remorse for having harmed or mistreated others. Sounds like our Belle, doesn't it?

Some forensic psychologists and social scientists opine the motivation of female serial killers differs from that of their male counterparts. The latter's motives are often seen as sadistic and driven by sexual urges, while women are more likely to murder for profit and for revenge. They are likely to kill in their homes or in such familiar places as where they work like hospitals and nursing homes. Male predators are most likely to hunt.

Belle's murders, at least of men, were for enhancing her social status and financial well-being. Revenge may have also been a factor. But why she killed all those children is much hazier.

Where Belle differs from the majority of female mass killers is that she used violent methods instead of poison, which was the typical way women dispatched their victims during that time period. Though Belle certainly liked her strychnine and arsenic, she employed such "male" methods as bludgeoning victims with heavy objects like hammers and axes. Her taste for dissection could also be viewed as a male trait.

The more I looked, the more I discovered. Belle collected pretty children; sometimes she had as many as twenty at a time in her Chicago home. Yet as much as she professed to love them, the majority disappeared never to be heard of again and at least two of them died. They were more like beautiful little toys, and once they became demanding or in some way offended her, she no longer wanted them around. Maybe, also, she had to make room for the next group of children and the money they would bring. Men sold their property and left home saying they were going to marry a rich widow in La Porte and were never heard from again. Women entered her home and never left. A peddler tied his wagon to her gate when she invited him in. He disappeared, but Belle—in an in-your-face move if there ever was one—added the horse and wagon to her stable. If the mailman arrived without any letters for her, she was angry. She was said to run several matrimonial agencies—another way to find victims.

Serial killers often act alone; that's their very nature. But by accepting that Belle was a businesswoman whose business was murder and insurance fraud, it becomes easier to believe she had at least one accomplice, Ray Lamphere, and probably another, Julius Truelson, a flawed and complicated man who had exact knowledge of the farm, including information not released by the police.

Belle's behaviors, if taken as business decisions, help us understand her actions. One important question is why, after the grueling poverty of her youth in rural Norway where her family made their living from subsistence farming, did Belle sell her lovely home in Chicago and move to a farm in rural Northwest Indiana? La Porte at that time, while quite nice, had a population of 7,113—shades of rural Norway from which she escaped. With all the insurance money from the deaths of her first husband, two children, and several fires, she could have lived well in the city. Instead, she traded that in to raise hogs and produce.

The home she purchased had once been owned by a madam from Chicago's notorious Levee District. The madam was connected to two powerful but extremely corrupt city aldermen who controlled the city's red-light district. Coincidence? Or a lucrative business move?

Lastly, evil and heartless as she was, Belle had amazing managerial and organizational skills. She wrote more than eighty letters to Andrew Helgelien alone over the eighteen months she was attempting to lure him to his death. In that time, she also kept up correspondence with other men, murdered and butchered some of them, ran her farm, slept with farmhands (she was an irresistible lover according to their accounts), raised her children, and made sure her products got to market.

Given all we know, Belle was more than a madwoman with a sharp knife. In some ways, she was a CEO, always ready to diversify her business model to make more money. She could easily have added running a body farm to her résumé. That would explain the many trunks and large boxes that arrived at her doorstep. The fancy cars pulling up to the farm late at night with young women as passengers and pretty ladies descending from trains arriving from Chicago at the La Porte depot and hiring hacks to take them to the farm after midnight likely indicated a side business of performing abortions.

There were times when I felt overwhelmed by so much information, much of it, though fascinating, seemingly unconnected. But the more I read and learned about Belle, the easier it was to connect the dots. Finally, when I found myself typing sentences such as "Asle Helgelien searched the property looking for where his brother Andrew might be buried," or "Joe Maxson and Daniel Hutson continued to search the rubble for the missing head of Belle Gunness" while eating a ham sandwich, I realized that I was completely engulfed by the story of Belle Gunness, having reached an understanding of who she was and what she did.

ACKNOWLEDGMENTS

WHEN I CALLED TED HARTZELL, A RESPECTED JOURNALIST who had written numerous articles about Belle Gunness both when he was a reporter for the *La Porte Herald-Argus* and then later for several magazines, he at first said he really hadn't thought about her for years but was willing to meet for coffee. I expected that since he was from La Porte, Indiana; had worked for the local paper there; and had written extensively about the case, I would get a few insights. Instead, Ted came in with a large banker's box, and when he took the lid off to show me the contents, I realized I was looking at the years of research he'd done on the case.

And he was turning it over to me.

What more can I say than thank you, Ted, and I promise to get that box back to you ASAP. Really, truly.

When historian Janet Langlois, PhD, started to write her book *Belle Gunness: The Lady Bluebeard*, she was aided by Lillian de la Torre, who several decades earlier had written her own book about the case. Lillian actively helped Janet by sharing her extensive research in exchange for the promise she would help another writer someday. Janet kept her promise by talking to me and sharing her notes and information. Janet was also there for me in other ways, providing counsel when I'd gathered facts that were baffling but compelling and assisting me in sorting them out to weave into the narrative I was creating. Thank you, Janet and Lillian.

Fern Eddy Schultz, who was officially designated by the State of Indiana as the La Porte County Historian and conducts her research at the La Porte County Historical Society in the Fern Eddy Schultz Research Library, named after her in honor of her years of dedication, doesn't like the focus on Belle. She sees La Porte as having so much more to offer than ghoulish stories about its most famous resident, but Fern helped me anyway, providing exceptional details about Elizabeth Smith, a totally fascinating character, and Sheriff Smutzer, another cipher in this case. Fern also gave me wonderful insight into what La Porte was like more than a century ago (hint: it's still as lovely as it was back then).

Andrea Simmons, an attorney and forensic anthropologist, spent several hours with me going over the details of her team's attempt to match up DNA of the bodies exhumed in 2009 from the Sorenson cemetery lot and from her soon-to-be-published book, which takes a scientific look at the crime.

Karin Rettinger and Anita Kopetski at the Marshall County Historical Society, who had helped me greatly on my book *Murders That Made Headlines: Crimes of Indiana*, again used their expert research skills in tracking down news stories on Johann Hoch and his victims Mary Schultz and her daughter, who were supposedly buried at Belle's.

Dale Hoppe, a friend for decades, since we were students at East Chicago Washington Public Schools, traveled to cemeteries taking excellent photos of the gravesites of Belle's victims.

Bruce Johnson, who wrote and starred in *The Gunness Mystery*, a popular and well-done movie directed by Stephen Ruminski, and who worked hard at bringing together the one-hundredth anniversary of remembrance of her crimes and helped find and restore headstones of her victims, took time to share his extensive knowledge of the crimes.

Suzie Richter, who retired as curator at the La Porte County Historical Society, was always a great help along with others on her staff, as was the museum's new director, Keri Teller Jakubowski.

Of course, a big thanks to Ashley Runyon, the former acquisitions editor at Indiana University Press who suggested I write about Belle, and to Anna C. Francis who guided me after Ashley left. I love you all as well as the entire team at Indiana University Press, including Nancy Lightfoot and David Hulsey.

A huge thanks to my editor. Lesley Bolton did a tremendous job editing my manuscripts and kept me on track when I went off on tangents. She made this book what it is, and I owe her big for that.

I give my love to my son, Evan, and an answer to my daughter, Nia, who asked me the other day when I was going to write about unicorns instead of murders: I will, I told her, when unicorns start murdering people.

And to my husband, John, a former prosecutor and a retired judge, I give an assurance: writing about murderers doesn't mean I have a penchant for committing murders. Honest.

Jane Simon Ammeson
February 2021

AMERICA's FEMME FATALE

1

Belle's Beginnings

BRYNHILD THOUGHT SHE'D FOUND LOVE IN DARKENED COR-
ners, in billows of hay in drafty old barns, and along the rocky
shore of Lake Selbu. At seventeen, Brynhild was healthy, tall, and
strong with fair skin and brilliant blue eyes; she was lusty and ven-
turesome as well. This combination had attracted the attention of
the son of a wealthy family, though history, unfortunately, doesn't
record his name.

She didn't mind when the cruel cold winds breezed through the
rotted slots of the barn or when the rocks on the beach bit into her
back when he roughly pushed her down. Because what he repre-
sented was more than a lusty, handsome young man; he was her
way out of the life she saw awaiting poor girls like her. She saw it
in her mother—haggard, bitter, aged like she was a hundred, with
nothing to look forward to but more never-ending hard work until
she finally took to her bed unable to go on anymore.

But now fate had taken a turn, and Brynhild saw a new future.
He was the favored son of a rich landowner, and one day, all those
acres, the fields of cattle, pens of pigs, and coops of chickens would
be his. He was her ticket to a better life, and even if he hadn't been
good looking or powerful and strong, she would have gone with him
anyway for all the money he would have one day.

As a result of their secret trysts, Brynhild had gotten what she
hoped for—she was pregnant, and now he would have to marry her.

As she went about her backbreaking chores on the family's rental plot of farmland, Brynhild imagined with anticipation what her days would become. Money would no longer be a constant worry, nor would she go hungry after a meager meal. She would sleep in a soft feather bed and have her servant stack as much hardwood into the roaring fireplace as she wanted. No longer would she have to rise early on freezing winter mornings, dress quickly in the cold, and walk through the snow to milk cows. Maybe best of all, she'd no longer need to gather snurkvist, the tiny dried-up twigs found on spruce trees, to try to keep the family warm during the cold Norwegian nights.

All that would be over. Or, it would be when she told him about the child, which she planned to do at the country dance on Saturday night. They would need to marry right away, before she started showing, before there could be talk.

Brynhild, who had long ago learned harsh truths, knew he wouldn't want to get married to a girl who collected snurkvist. He always avoided her in public, particularly when he was with his friends. And she'd seen him talking to the daughter of a wealthy farmer. If not for her baby, he would most likely grow tired of her and marry someone of his own class, casting her aside. Or he would marry and still expect Brynhild to yield to him when he wanted. That was the way of men.

But now he didn't have a choice. He couldn't deny the child. Her child, *his* child, would be her salvation.

Brynhild ran a hand over her hard stomach, allowing herself just a moment to linger in daydream. With a sigh, she turned her attention back to the cows. It would soon be time to drive them back to the farm for the evening milking.

Later, as she made cheese from fresh milk, she had another brief thought. It flitted through her brain, just lingering for a second. Suppose once she was his wife, just suppose that something happened to his father. A farm mishap maybe—after all, they were common enough—or an affliction of some sort. It wasn't right to think such things, she told herself. But then Brynhild always did, wishing the girls who laughed at her overly mended hand-me-downs and her old leather boots with the split seams might be sickened by cholera or typhoid, those diseases that carried off people from the village. It was just a thought, she repeated to herself. Thinking didn't make it real. But, oh, if all those pigs were hers.

On Saturday evening, Brynhild donned her best dress wishing it didn't look so patched and worn, brushed and braided her hair while admiring its lustrous shine, and envisioned the scene ahead of her with a small smile. What could go wrong, she thought. She held all the cards.

At the dance, she ignored the snide calls of "Snurkvistpala," the nickname given to her because her family was too poor to afford hardwood for their fire. Whispering to herself, You'll see, she passed by, not letting it bother her as it had before. Soon they wouldn't dare call her such a name.

Anxiously she looked around until she spotted him. He was moving toward a gathering of friends—his friends, not hers. She intercepted him before they noticed his arrival.

She whispered her need to speak with him.

He did not answer, only turned his back to her. He was angry, she knew, because she had broken their rule. No, not their rule, *his* rule. He had always set the perimeters of their relationship. He would not do so anymore.

She straightened her tall frame, making sure that her breasts pulled at the fabric of her dress, and she caught his appreciative gape. Hissing now, she threatened that if he didn't go with her, she'd loudly say her piece right then and there, nodding toward the group to ensure he took her point. He got it. Though he didn't answer her, he headed toward a side door. Normally, when he signaled he wanted to meet her outside, Brynhild dared not follow closely. She was quite adept at slipping through shadows for their secret couplings without being seen. After all, she'd be ruined if people knew about them. But now, did it really matter? She smiled triumphantly as she walked past those who had been too good for her before this.

Outside, in the cold, under black skies lit by just a few stars, he turned to face her, annoyed and impatient. Their relationship was on his terms, not hers. Ill at ease with his stare, Brynhild blurted out that she was pregnant. It wasn't quite how she had intended to share the news, but it hit the mark.

He stepped back against the building quickly as if shoved. He was quiet for just a moment, then recovered quickly. He laughed and shrugged, simply refuting the child was his.

However, Brynhild was not a woman to be denied and said as much. She had too much at stake.

His laughter stopped, and a murderous rage crossed his face. He wouldn't marry her, child or no child, he told her. His parents would object; they wanted a good match, and so did he. His time with Brynhild was for what she aroused in him. That was not love any more than was what rutting animals did in heat.

I will tell everyone the truth, she hissed. I will go to your parents, I will go to the church, I will tell everyone, and you will have to marry me.

He sneered, and despite all his anger, he had enough control to keep his voice low when he asked, How do I even know it's mine? Who knows how many men you lift your skirts for.

Even in the dark shadows, she saw a realization cross his face, and the words he said next were chilling: I have enough friends who will say they used you too, that you were always willing to go with anyone and even asked for money afterward, he said with an imperious smirk. He was, after all, a rich, spoiled man who never had to take responsibility for his own actions.

His words were cruel, and she almost shrank back. But even as she listened to him, she felt herself harden. He would not get away with this—no matter what, she would get even. But she also felt her dream of life as the wife of a rich man morphing into the nightmare of a woman shunned by all, even her family, left on her own to care for herself and a small child. Shocked and panicked, Brynhild started to argue, her voice growing louder. She was so enraged and so scared, she didn't realize the extent of his fury until he swung a fist, hitting her hard in the stomach. She bent over in pain, expecting him to stop. But he didn't. His blows were brutal and drove her to the ground.

You're a whore, he said as he kicked at her middle, where her— no, *their*—baby lived, several times before turning away and walking back into the dance hall. As the door opened, she heard the sounds of laughter and music and his final words: I don't want you or your bastard baby. When I have a child, he will be of good stock by a girl from a good family. No poor farm family like yours.

She lay on the ground in agony, not yet able to even pull herself up, and then she felt the blood starting to flow between her legs.

Her child was dying, right there as she lay in the dirt in the back of the barn. She watched the rivulets of blood seeping down her legs spill onto the dark ground. Her child was dying and with it her power over him and her chance for the life she wanted so badly. She heard voices approach and somehow was able to pull herself away from the light of the door when it opened. She was in the dark as a couple came out, laughing. Thankfully, they didn't stop but continued up toward the woods where she knew there was a soft bed of pine needles where they could lay. Not long before, she and her lover had done the same thing.

Brynhild felt herself losing consciousness and knew she needed to get away, to go home, and so half crawling and half walking, she made her way, the blood coming faster. Then, a sharp and sudden pain made her fall again. She could feel the discharge, her baby, leave her body. Despite her pain, her humiliation, her overwhelming sadness, she knew what she must do. With her bare hands, she scraped away the almost-frozen earth to lay the tiny remains of her future in the soil.

And then, she continued on, her journey more difficult since she couldn't take the road; she didn't want anyone to see her like this. What would people think if they came across her now?

But, of course, she knew the answer to that. They'd think the raggedy Snurkvistpala had gotten herself in trouble and gotten just what she deserved for reaching too high. They'd ask each other, Who did she think she was?

Brynhild would get home no matter how long it took. She wouldn't let herself die in the cold. She'd climb into the bed she shared with her sisters and not say a word. She would not cry anymore. Crying did no good; it made you weak.

And I will never be weak again, she told herself over and over. She felt the cold seeping into her body and knew that if she didn't keep moving, she would perish on the path in the woods leading toward home.

Afterward, Brynhild couldn't remember how she made the last mile home that night or how she managed to stuff rags between her legs to stop the bleeding. She put another one in her mouth to keep any sobs from escaping. She didn't sleep but instead wondered, as she listened to her sisters' light snores, how it had all gone so terribly wrong. She felt waves of anguish pass through her body at the thought of having to endure her life on the farm after coming so close to the life she wanted, a life of ease and comfort, a life of the ways of those with money. She dreaded the thought of that blond girl he had been flirting with getting her cows, pigs, chickens, and her man. How would she bear seeing them together, happy? And why did that girl deserve his wealth? Her father was already wealthy enough. Whereas Brynhild had nothing. She knew her reputation would be gone now. Would any good young man have her? Or would she need to marry a drunken lout with few acres and a disinclination to work.

Finally, the spasms and bleeding stopped. It was almost dawn now and the cows awaited, probably already mooing loudly as their udders became uncomfortably full. She solaced herself with a vow. She'd do whatever was necessary to have money, fine clothes, and a nice house—no matter what. And she would have revenge.

One day as she was herding the cows up into the high meadow, she saw her lover talking to friends. They all turned to look at her. He gave her a smile, condescending and cold. She stopped short and looked at him and then each of the men with him, and she smiled back. But there was evil in her smile and a burning warning in her eyes, and they all saw that. Their talking stopped, and they looked away. Brynhild saw one of the men finger the trollkors, or troll cross, a bent piece of iron that many wore to ward off evil and protect against black magic.

If I wanted to, she thought, no trollkors would stop me from harming you.

But she didn't want to hurt that man. She wouldn't waste her time with him. There was only one of that group that would pay for what had happened to her and her baby. She started walking again with the cows, but she didn't hear the men begin talking again. They were still, she was sure, staring after her, still fearful of the smile they had seen on her face.

Shortly after that encounter, Brynhild's lover became extremely ill. She heard from his family's servants how he lay in bed, vomiting and retching, his pain so intense he said he wanted to die.

Stomach cancer was what many thought when he, in the throes of torment, finally died. But there were some who saw the faint smile of satisfaction play across Brynhild's lips as her lover's body was made ready for burial and wondered otherwise.

As for her lover, did he, on his deathbed, wonder if Brynhild had had her revenge? Had she somehow poisoned him? Those who knew Brynhild thought so, and soon gossip decreed this to be Brynhild's first murder.

Selbu was a small, poor, fishing and farming village, and the Storset family—Paul Pedersen Storset and Berit Olsdatter and their eight children, of whom Brynhild Paulsdatter Storset, born on November 11, 1859, was youngest—were among the poorest. They tilled a small plot of leased land on the Størsetgjerdet farm. Selbu was an isolated village. Trondheim, the largest city in central Norway, about thirty-seven miles away, was a port city located where the river Nidelva emptied into the Trondheim Fjord, an inlet of the Norwegian Sea.

This far north, the weak winter light lasted for just four hours or even less, and the sun seldom emerged from the blanket of clouds. Predictably, winters were very bitter and cold. Even in the heat of summer, the temperature rarely made it into the upper sixties, but still, that was a joyful time as crops ripened and children could take a bucket and collect sweet berries growing wild, eating as many as their stomachs could hold.

Paul and Berit owned little, just two cows, three sheep, one goat, and their meager household goods and tattered clothes. The paltry yield from their crops averaged one-eighth of a Norwegian tonne (a metric ton) of barley, one-half tonne of oats, and about 220 pounds of potatoes. In comparison, a more typical farm in the area had two horses, twelve cattle, fifteen sheep, nine goats, and one pig, and produced five and a quarter tonnes of seed corn and five tonnes of potatoes.

To supplement the family's income, Paul worked as a stone mason as well, particularly during the winter when there was less to do on the farm. Despite the extra work, the Storset family was often in dire need and once even qualified for the poor fund.

Farm life meant almost endless hard work, and like her siblings, Brynhild labored from early morning to late evening. The list of tasks was long and included tilling, planting, weeding, harvesting, milking, churning, cooking, caring for animals, cleaning, and mending. For families like the Storsets, hard work started at a young age, and before she turned fourteen years old, Brynhild found employment at another farm as well. Working as a cattle girl, her duties included milking the cows in the morning before herding them up into higher pastures where she kept them under observation, ensuring they didn't wander off and weren't attacked by wild animals. At the end of the day, tired from chasing after wandering bovines, she'd drive the cattle back to the farm. Then it was time for milking one more time. Only once the cows were secure and safe for the night could Brynhild think about rest—that is, unless she needed to churn cream into butter and cheese to fill her employer's larder.

When her chores were done and if she wasn't too tired, Brynhild might sit in one of the darkened cottages with other women, the only light and warmth coming from a stove or fireplace. While knitting or sewing, they would amuse themselves by gossiping or discussing the supernatural threats rural Norwegians often believed plagued the countryside.

These tales weren't meant to entertain as much as they were warnings to the innocent who must always be on the alert against vile spirits in human disguise bent on wickedness—as real and as dangerous as any wild animal roaming at night. Brynhild listened with fascination to stories about trolls, witches, river sprites, clever beasts, and hill spirits. Everywhere, warned the stories, humans were being seduced into their demise. Brynhild paid attention and learned. Even as a child, she already knew life could be cruel and harsh. Perhaps the stories held the answer to escape—only the strong, the swift, the powerful survived.

Even though superstitions ran deep, education was compulsory in Norway, and Brynhild did well in school. One teacher described her as clever, and indeed the future would prove that to be very true. Her employer would later say she was well behaved and diligent, and her pastor recalled her as a good girl with higher-than-average intelligence.

But sometimes up in the mountains, away from the setting of a formal education and alone with the cows, she thought about the stories the women told as they knitted mittens with the distinctive snowflake pattern that is even now a tradition in Selbu. Everywhere, according to the tales, evil waited, often in the guise of beauty. The lovely music coming from Nakk's harp cast such an enchantment that his listeners followed him into the river and were swept away. With her beauty, Hulder, the female land version of Nakk, lured men into her underground lair, never to return.

With the rustle of the wind in the grasses, Brynhild often looked around, wondering if one-eyed or multiple-headed trolls were creeping up in hopes of feasting on her blood. The sound of a horse in the distance when she wasn't expecting anyone might signal the upcoming arrival of the ghostly Nix astride her magnificent white horse. She must be strong, she thought, and resist the impulse to follow Nix up higher into the mountains, where she would disappear forever.

What would be worse, Brynhild wondered. Perhaps drowning after following Nakk into the river would be merciful compared to what the vanished, trapped forever in an underground lair, might endure. She shivered and focused on her dreams—a wealthy husband and a life of comfort. Whatever it took.

Many people in Selbu were receiving letters from relatives, neighbors, and friends who had immigrated to America. They wrote of all the opportunities available there. If Brynhild couldn't have her handsome, wealthy lover in Norway, perhaps America would prove more accommodating.

Brynhild's older sister, Olina Storset, had left Norway and settled in Chicago. There she had Americanized her name to Nellie and married a fellow Norwegian named John R. Olson. He generously purchased a ticket for his sister-in-law.

With no regrets, twenty-one-year-old Brynhild packed her meager belongings and said her goodbyes. Though she hugged her parents and siblings and promised to write, she did not spare one glance back at the farm. Those crossing the ocean rarely saw their Norway homes and loved ones again—the distance and the cost were too great. Many pined for their homeland for the remainder of their lives—Brynhild would learn to take advantage of that. In the years to come, Brynhild's life, both in Norway and in America, would be examined, and everything about her that could be found analyzed endlessly and discussed over and over. Letters she'd written to others were read and reread, but no one ever seems to have found a letter she'd written home. She was done with Norway. She was on to her next adventure.

It took four days by boat to get from Trondheim to Kingston upon Hull in England across the North Sea. If the waters were calm, there was music and dancing on deck. But passage to England was more often rough and wild, the boat rising and falling as it navigated large rolling waves. Strong winds tugged at clothing and blew hats over the railing, while cold salt water soaked those on deck. Many became desperately seasick, splattering vomit on the decks, a slippery hazard for those who stepped in it and might fall or, at best, soil their clothes and shoes, where it would remain until they landed and could find somewhere to wash. Despite this, being above deck was often better than being below, where the rocking motion was even more severe, objects became deadly missiles as the boat rose and fell, and the air was stale and rank.

Landfall brought about an overwhelming sense of relief. From Hull, passengers made their way to Liverpool, where they boarded a vessel for an even longer trip across the Atlantic. But Brynhild was lucky because by the 1880s, the trip took only about two weeks or so, compared to years earlier when the voyage lasted over a month and sometimes even longer. The ship she took, possibly the *Tasso*, was the nineteenth-century version of a hybrid, using sails as well as a steam engine.

Diaries of passengers from that time record how rough and deadly the journey could be. Deaths aboard weren't uncommon. Women suffered in childbirth. A leak meant that passengers had to bail. Rudimentary meals were covered in the price of the ticket, and passengers with money could buy extras from the captain and crew. There was no refrigeration or even much storage, so provisions often became waterlogged or infested with bugs. Bad food meant dysentery; strong winds and waves meant a pitching boat. It didn't take long for the few but much-needed privies to overflow. Close quarters meant that contagious diseases like measles and chicken pox spread quickly.

After long days of travel under these conditions and sleeping at night in cramped quarters with dirty, tired, and life-worn strangers, Brynhild descended into the chaos of travelers disembarking from many ships from many lands arriving in their new country.

Immigrants arriving from Europe after a lengthy and sometimes dangerous voyage across the Atlantic Ocean. *Photo courtesy of Library of Congress.*

She wondered, as she held her bag tightly and stepped onto the dock in New York City, if leaving the open-air fields of Selbu had been the right decision. Everything was so different. She had come from a small village, and now, just on the docks, the sights, smells, scenes, and cacophony of many languages were overwhelming. She was only one of thousands who seemed lost and scared. But she steeled herself, pushing her way to the long line snaking toward the immigration clerks. As she moved slowly forward, Brynhild tried to brush the stains and dirt off her dress and patted her braided hair into place. There were no bathing facilities aboard the ship, and she was aware of how bedraggled and dirty she must look.

She smiled and nodded at the clerk who looked over her papers, but she didn't understand what he was saying in his rapid English. And he didn't understand a word of Norwegian. Nor did many people, she learned, when she tried to find her way to the station to board a train for Chicago. Finally, she found her way and settled into third class, still clutching her bag—she didn't want to lose it; after all, it was all she had.

On her way, any thoughts of returning home disappeared. What would she be going back to? Gossip had her a murderess, so at best her option would be to marry a poor farmer and work herself ragged. As she looked out the window at the passing landscape, so different from Norway, she thought it better to go forward rather than back.

2

Life and Death in Chicago

WHEN SHE ARRIVED IN CHICAGO, THE FAMILIAR FACE OF HER sister helped bring Brynhild's resolve even further into focus. Olina—rather, Nellie, as she was now called—looked so elegant in her fine clothes walking accompanied by her prosperous-looking husband, who had enough money and was kind enough to pay for his sister-in-law's ticket to America. The two sisters hugged, and for the first time in a long while, Brynhild felt affection in her heart. Nellie looped her arm through her sister's and walked her from the platform. Nellie's husband, John, carried Brynhild's tattered bag containing what few possessions she had.

Brynhild couldn't hide her amazement as she stepped out into the grand city of Chicago. The city stretched on and on, both outward and upward. Horses, cable cars, and people all vied for space on the city streets. The din created was nearly maddening but was at the same time exciting. The city held promises that could never have been imagined in a small Norwegian village. The fastest-growing city at the time, Chicago's population was slightly over half a million. Lured by the rise in industry and commerce, immigrants poured in from all over Europe, especially English, Germans, Swedes, Dutch, and Norwegians.

When the trio arrived at the door to Nellie and John's house, Brynhild looked around at the sights and listened to the sounds, surprised to be reminded of the little village she'd left behind. She

Belle Gunness with Jennie Olsen (standing) and Myrtle
Sorenson. *Photo courtesy of La Porte County Historical
Society.*

could hear, above the traffic, people speaking Norwegian, and from
a nearby bakery, she smelled freshly baked oatmeal molasses bread
her mother used to make. Nellie and John lived in a Norwegian
neighborhood where the customs and traditions of the homeland
were still closely followed. Norwegian housewives cooked and
served the foods their mothers and grandmothers taught them to
make. They and their families attended churches where services
were conducted in Norwegian, they frequented stores where goods
from their homeland were sold, and they saw doctors, store clerks,
and others in their everyday lives who also were from their country

and spoke the language. Many still even wore Drakter, traditional special garments, to dances and other gatherings.

Indeed, Brynhild wasn't alone in a strange land here in her sister's neighborhood. Between 1825 and 1925, 2.1 million Scandinavians immigrated to America. While the majority were Swedes, Norway sent a greater percentage of its population. Approximately one million Norwegians left their country between 1820 and 1920. And here, in what was known as Little Norway, she joined a large settlement of Norwegians, many from rural areas such as hers.

"A newcomer from Norway who arrives here will be surprised indeed to find in the heart of the country, more than a thousand miles from his landing place, a town where language and way of life so unmistakably remind him of his native land," wrote Svein Nilsson, a Norwegian American journalist, in *Billed-Magazine*, on May 14, 1870.

Brynhild didn't speak English, and she wouldn't have to—she could live her entire life in this neighborhood and never hear a word spoken in any language other than Norwegian. She could even follow the news and events by reading *Skandinaven*, a Norwegian-language newspaper founded in Chicago in 1866. Around the time Brynhild moved to Chicago, it was the largest Norwegian-language journal in the world—even bigger than any newspaper in Norway.

Dishes from the homeland were served in the dining rooms of friends and family and at church dinners and other social events: home-brewed ale made from malt, molasses, or sugarcane; flatbrød (flatbread); smultringer (doughnuts); and rømmegrøt, a cream porridge. People in the streets would have asked, "Hvordan sta'r det til?" (How are you?), and she would have responded, "Bare bra" (Just fine, thanks). And so, though Brynhild was leaving behind her family and friends never to return, she would be enveloped in all things Norwegian, with the stark exception of Norway itself.

But Brynhild hadn't traveled all this way to simply live the same life in a larger—albeit much larger—village. She wanted to change her life, and to start, she gave herself a new name: Bella.

Nellie lived in a comfortable house, with nice furniture, rugs, and paintings. She had five children and a girl who came in to help clean. She was so proud of her children that she talked about them all the time, which soon grated on Bella's nerves. But Bella did find

Nellie's youngest child, a sweet little girl named Olga, to have a very pretty face and pretty manners. At times, if she let herself think about the baby she had lost, she felt both an overwhelming sadness and also an anger, not just at the child's father but at the unfairness of life. She should have—and she would have, she vowed—the happy homelife that Nellie had.

Olga would sit on Bella's lap, and Bella would read stories to the sweet little girl while stroking her soft, silky hair. "I love you, Aunt Bella," Olga would say, and Bella felt happy. But when she heard Olga say the same words to her mother, father, and siblings, Bella felt resentment and even a sense of rejection—as if Olga were betraying her. Those feelings caused her to seethe and again recall all the wrongs that had been done to her. Why should Nellie have all this and she need to be dependent on her sister's and John's kindness?

But Bella had plans. She could stay at Nellie's as there was room in the house, but she would need to find a job and contribute to the family coffers for her food and board. And so like many young Norwegian women who immigrated, she first took a job as a domestic. That would do until she met a man with money. And then there would be more babies. Or so she hoped.

Sometimes Bella worried that someone in Selbu who knew her sister would write a letter, telling Nellie of the suspicions that were being whispered about Bella's lover's death. But she never felt bad about what had happened to him. He had killed their child and maybe had hoped she would die as well. She still shivered when she thought of that cold, bloody crawl back home.

Though she knew she should be grateful for the work—it was so much easier than milking cows in the frigid winters—jealousy overwhelmed her as she swept floors, washed fine china dishes, changed linens, and hung rich tapestries out on the clothesline to swat the dust out. Some of the women rose late, well after Bella had been toiling for hours and after their husbands had left for work. Some of these women were nice, but others were demanding, complaining that Bella hadn't swept the fireplace clean enough or the silver didn't shine.

Bella also marveled at how some had let their looks go, their figures now plump, the gray showing in their hair, and their faces void of even a little rouge. Didn't they worry that their husbands would find younger and prettier women to spend their time with? Of course, a few of the men did, noticing the trim ankles and the attractiveness of the tall, strong, blue-eyed housemaid as she climbed onto a chair to take the feather duster to the chandelier and catching the rise of her large bosom as she took deep breaths after working extra hard. She enjoyed their looks, and if they wanted to give her trinkets or slip some extra money into her apron, so be it.

And so gifts were passed and time was stolen when the wives were elsewhere. She liked the money and gifts very much, as well as the hurried, passionate sex. Surprisingly, though the attack and miscarriage were so awful, she was always passionate and always ready. Men were amazed at her vitality and enthusiasm. But even more than the encounters, she liked knowing when a wife made a demand or criticized her that she had slept with her husband. It made her feel superior. She loved secrets, and she loved knowing that she had the power, with just a few words, to ruin these women's happiness and security. Just knowing was enough. At least for now.

Bella never shied from hard work, and she took on as much as she possibly could. Even so, she made time for socializing at neighborhood picnics and other such gatherings, always with an eye toward possible suitors. There were many men at the dances, but the one who caught her eye was fellow Norwegian Mads Ditlev Anton Sorenson. Mads was handsome, broad-shouldered, and a bit taller than Bella's nearly six-foot frame.

Five years Bella's senior, Mads had a steady job as a night watchman at Mandel Bros., one of Chicago's leading department stores, and a gentle nature. He doted on Bella and promised to give her everything she wanted. The couple married in 1884, when Bella was twenty-five years old.

Mads was crazy about Bella and tried to fulfill her dreams. He set her up in a comfortable apartment, provided her with jewels and clothes, and did all he could to satisfy her demands. Still, Bella felt she was missing out—she wanted more money and also children.

She continued the affairs with her employers and pocketed the money after their many kisses and fondling. But she still felt aggrieved. Why did Nellie have such a happy and healthy brood of five while Bella had none? She scowled when she saw a mother on the streets with a passel of adorable young children. She deserved, more than those mothers, pretty babes who would tell her how much they loved her. It was hardly fair.

Bella, remembering the child she had lost, thought if she could only have a daughter like Nellie's youngest—the pretty and sweet Olga—she would be happy at last. Of course, it hadn't worked out very well when Olga had come to stay with Bella for a week or so. Bella had gotten cranky at some of the things Olga did, and when other children wanted to play with the new girl on their block, Bella said no. She wanted Olga all to herself. Olga, upset, pouted, even stamping her little feet, and Bella raised her hand as if to hit her. That was too much for Olga, and she started crying. When Mads came home, she was still sobbing, and so Mads, who had the softest heart, took her home, returning to Bella's wrath.

She has to learn to obey! Bella yelled at him. She is so spoiled that even though I made her treats every day and bought her things, she still talked about wanting to play with the Larson twins down the street. She is ungrateful.

Mads, as was usual for him when Bella began to yell, retreated into the parlor with his newspaper, trying to tune her out. He knew it was useless to argue. Nothing could assuage Bella's anger when she was in one of her moods. Unfortunately, he thought, remembering the smiling, flirtatious woman he had first met and courted, those moods were almost constant. Nothing was ever good enough.

Bella thought it would be different if Olga came to live with her. It would make life perfect, and maybe John and Nellie would give her some extra money for caring for the doll-like little girl. Nellie was always complaining about how busy her children kept her, and she did indeed look so tired when Bella stopped to visit toward the end of the day. Bella decided she would help out; she would take Olga to live with her.

One afternoon as the children played in the small garden, Bella lay her head in Nellie's lap and sighed deeply, lamenting that she was still barren, that no child was growing inside of her. Nellie stroked Bella's hair and worried over her unhappiness, plying her with encouraging words—she and Mads had only been married a short time, after all. But Bella was adamant in her belief that she could not have children.

As the two women commiserated, Bella talked of her love for Olga, describing her as the perfect child, so sweet and warm and pretty. She talked about how she felt a connection with her niece that she'd not felt with any other human being. With tear-stained cheeks, Bella asked her older sister if she could adopt her youngest child. Nellie, shocked that her sister would dare ask such a thing, sat up so abruptly that Bella almost fell to the ground. No, she said, outraged at the suggestion.

Through her fury, Bella could not see why she was being denied this opportunity for happiness. Nellie, she told her, could always have more children, but this might be—probably would be—her only chance to know a child's love. How dare Nellie keep that from her?

Cajoling became cursing, but Nellie again refused. She did not say it, but she remembered when Olga had gone to stay with her aunt Bella and how she had pleaded to come home early. Olga was too young to totally explain why she felt so uneasy with Aunt Bella, but Nellie could see how upset and afraid she was.

Also, though she hadn't mentioned it to Bella, both she and John had received letters from people they knew in Selbu. The letters told stories about the pregnancy and the agonizing death of the rich farmer's son. Nellie believed they were just ugly rumors from people jealous that Bella had been able to come to America. This was her sister, Nellie told herself, and she would never do anything like that.

John didn't say anything to contradict Nellie. Blood was thick, he told himself. He also had heard stories from men who knew the men Bella worked for. They were salacious tales told in the bars when John stopped by for a drink after work. The men told of his sister-in-law hiking her skirts up and bending over the kitchen table for husbands when the wife and kids were away in exchange for money or other things of value. And he had watched as Bella manipulated her sister with her sad stories. He had come to believe Bella was capable of doing exactly what the letter writers said.

So no, neither husband nor wife would let Olga go live with Bella.

Besides, Nellie was the girl's mother and she loved her. She should grow up with her own family. Children weren't just objects to be lent out. Sometimes Nellie wondered if Bella was able to under-stand other people's feelings or if she was so wrapped up in her own concerns that she didn't care about anything but getting what she wanted. She really hadn't known Bella that well because she left for America when her sister was still so very young. But even then Bella had been argumentative, defiant, and headstrong. Sadly, it seemed she really hadn't changed much after all those years.

When Nellie refused again to let Olga live with Bella, the younger sister was incensed and quickly left the house, making sure to slam the door so hard that a pretty vase on the mantel toppled to the floor, splintering into pieces. Nellie didn't know it then, but whatever bond the two sisters had forged in this new land was forever broken. Very rarely after that did Bella come to visit or even speak to Nellie. It saddened Nellie, but she would find out in the years to come that she had probably saved Olga's life.

In 1890, Bella found an opportunity in tragedy. The wife of Mads's good friend Anton Olsen was dying, leaving behind several children, including a blond, blue-eyed eight-month-old baby named Jennie—one of the sweetest and prettiest infants Bella had ever seen. Rushing right over to the house, Bella made a huge fuss over the bedridden woman. She moved about the house, cleaning, caring for the children, and making supper to feed them all. As she brought a bit of broth to the woman's cracked lips, Bella lamented that she did not have the means to take care of the whole family but stated that she could certainly help out with the youngest. In front of Anton, Bella begged his dying wife to let her raise little Jennie. The woman, with all the hopes a dying mother could have for her child, put the infant in Bella's arms, making her swear to raise the child as her own. Of course, Bella said, she would, declaring she would love her like her own. Anton did not protest as it was an arrangement that worked to his benefit as well. Anton was an engineer and had several other children to raise. An infant could not be properly cared for without his wife. But he made it clear that this was temporary. He took Bella aside as she was holding the smiling baby and whispered to her as he did not want his wife to hear. When the shock of his wife's death was past and he was more settled, maybe even remarried, he would want Jennie back, he told Bella.

Of course, Bella promised, looking down at the babe, who had made no fuss when placed in her arms. But till then, I will treat her like my own, she told him.

Now that she had the baby, she wanted to leave right away, but she knew it wouldn't be right to take the child out of the house while the mother still lived. Though she was impatient, she hid those feelings. When the mother died, Bella almost let out a sigh of relief but was able to catch herself in time.

Bella beamed as she carried the baby in her arms back to the little apartment she shared with her loving husband. She looked around as she stepped inside. They would need a bigger place—a house, with a big yard, perhaps a few ponies—but this would require much more money than they were bringing in. How could she get the money they needed? Bella couldn't go to work now that she had a baby at home to care for. She would have to find another way to supplement Mads's earnings.

And besides, just one child wasn't enough. She wanted more.

The Norwegian community frequently hosted picnics in parks such as Humboldt Park for orphaned and underprivileged children, and Bella liked to attend. She would speak to the crowd, offering to take children into her care when parents needed a break or to even adopt unwanted children. Bella's obsession with children was partly to blame, but so was the commercial business of child adoption.

In Chicago, baby farming was big business. Maternity hospitals charged unmarried mothers for disposing of unwelcome infants. Those hospitals could then turn another profit by selling the unwanted child to parents interested in adoption. After all, as one slogan stated, "It's cheaper and easier to buy a baby for $100 than to have one of your own." Orphanages also trafficked in children.

At times, Bella would have as many as ten or twelve children living in her home. Some of these children came from overcrowded orphanages that paid people like Bella large amounts of money to adopt unwanted children. Some adoptions were more casual, and parents unable to care for their children simply turned them over to Bella.

Bella loved and doted on the children for a while but quickly grew tired of the constant care they required, and of the several children who entered the home, very few were ever documented as leaving even though they were no longer seen around. Of course, infant mortality rates were quite high in the 1890s.

Humboldt Park, Chicago. *Photo courtesy of Chicago Architecture Center.*

One such child was named Lucy. Little Lucy was thirteen months old when she went to live with Bella. By all accounts, the sweet child was just darling, and she made an impression on all who visited the Sorenson home—so much so that questions arose when, a year later, Lucy was gone. Bella was vague in her assurances; the child was simply returned to the wealthy parents from whom Bella had secured her, she would say, offering no further details. But, in a way that foretold Bella's future lies, she told others that Lucy had been sent to live at an institution. She would not answer questions of when, where, or to whom the child was sent. And the tone of her voice made it clear that she wanted no more questions asked. Women who had lost children marveled that Bella showed no sadness or concern that the adorable little girl who had lived there for a year was gone.

Don't you miss her? one rather bold woman asked. Bella's response was to fix her with a look, and the other woman turned away.

Her attitude inflamed the already raging whispers about Lucy's disappearance. Some spoke of nefarious deeds. Bella ignored them and felt she owed no one an explanation. With the lack of documentation required for fostering or adoption, no one could prove Bella a liar. No one knew Lucy's last name or even if Lucy was really her first name. But they missed the little girl and worried about what had really happened to her.

Bella's vision of wealth was coming together but slowly, too slowly. Mads was a hard worker, but he didn't earn enough to suit his wife. The money Bella made from foster care and adoptions and occasional visits to the homes of her former employers when their families were gone helped some, but it was not nearly enough. She was determined to take a more active role in achieving her version of the American dream.

All around, people were making fortunes by taking advantage of Chicago's expanding industry and commerce. The Sorensons had a little money from a house-fire insurance payout. Bella felt she had a head for business and convinced Mads to use the money to purchase a small confectionery store on the corner of Elizabeth Street and Grand Avenue. Besides sweets, the store also sold cigars, tobacco, newspapers, grocery staples, stationery, and popular candies such as William Wrigley Jr.'s Juicy Fruit Chewing Gum, Wrigley's Spearmint Chewing Gum, Good & Plenty, butterscotch-flavored Reed's Rolls, taffy, candy corn, and Red Bird Soft Peppermint Puffs.

Things moved quickly after this purchase. While the candy shop did not bring in the wealth Bella imagined—it was by all accounts a failure—it was a move that propelled the couple forward and increased their finances in a somewhat different and less ethical manner. The confectionary hadn't been open for even a year when it burned to the ground. Only Bella and Jennie, just three years old, were on the premises at the time. Jennie was slightly burned, though Bella was unharmed. Bella told insurers that a small kerosene lamp had exploded and started the blaze. Such a lamp was never found in the rubble, but the insurance was paid.

Bella and Mads used this money to move to the outskirts of Austin, Illinois, at the time a well-to-do Chicago suburb. Mads quickly got a job with the Chicago and North Western Railroad. Having moved up in the world due to fire, Bella realized that hard work and marriage were not the only means to the end she longed for.

In the same year, one of the Sorenson children, three-month-old Caroline, suddenly died, and Bella again collected on insurance. The death was attributed to acute colitis; however, the symptoms of acute colitis shared those of poisoning: fever, diarrhea, nausea, and abdominal cramping. Suspicions were kept to a whisper, but neighbors began to take note of the strange woman who had visitors in the dead of night and new foster children the next morning. Though several children came to the Sorenson household, Bella and Mads gave only four their name: Caroline, Axel, Myrtle, and Lucy. Jennie kept her family name of Olsen—most likely so Anton didn't get suspicious that Bella had no plans to ever let her return to her biological family. Many declared that none really belonged to Bella; even Jennie had never been legally adopted.

In 1898, neighborhood talk rose and became fevered because the Sorensons suffered yet another fire and another infant death. This time, five-month-old Axel followed little Caroline to the cemetery. He too was said to have died from acute colitis; he too had life insurance, and the company paid again.

Bella was inconsolable, and as Mads tried to comfort her, she recounted how tragedy followed her everywhere. How could one woman live with so much loss? What would she and the children do if Mads also died; how would they survive?

Mads had come to realize that everything was about Bella. He had buried both Caroline and Axel and felt so much pain. He had loved little Lucy, delighting when she held up her arms to him when he came home after a hard day. He always found time, no matter how tired he was, to play with the children, to read them a book, and to walk the floor with the two babies when they cried in pain as they were dying. Sometimes Bella slept through their cries. But Mads couldn't, wouldn't. He held them and tried to help ease their discomfort even though it meant not getting to sleep until late or not at all. It didn't matter that he'd be so tired at work. Someone needed to help those little children.

It was odd, but when Caroline got ill, Mads was so worried and he was sure, so sure, that she wouldn't live, but he didn't know why. It was just a feeling. He felt the same way when Axel became ill. Again, it was that feeling, call it a premonition, that no matter what he or the doctor or the good neighbors did, Axel would die too. And he was right.

Bella didn't care about his sorrow and absolute sense of loss when those little bodies were laid in the ground or when there was no Lucy to hold up her arms to him when he came home. It was always about Bella. Sometimes he wondered if she loved him or the children or anyone but herself.

Mads was also concerned with their new renter. He had liked Peter Gunness when he first moved in. It wasn't unusual for them to take in boarders, and Peter, who had recently emigrated from Norway, was just in Chicago for a short time to earn money, and then he would move in with his family in Wisconsin. A good-looking blonde with strong shoulders and a pleasant manner, Peter was a pleasure to talk with over the dinner table. But then Mads started noticing how friendly Bella was with the younger man, how she cooked all the Norwegian dishes he loved. A couple of times, Peter came home early from work before Mads got home. Mads noticed there was something in the air, he couldn't quite place it, between his wife and their boarder. But Mads was so decent it was difficult for him to believe ill of others, and he shook those feelings off and was genuinely sad to see Peter move away.

Bella fussed about Mads's health, worrying about his enlarged heart and lamenting that he was getting older. What would happen to her and the children if he died? she wailed. Her despair was contagious, and when Mads joined the North American Union, he signed his application and took out another, larger insurance policy to ensure his family was well taken care of should his heart give out.

The last home of Belle and her first husband, Mads Sorenson, in the Chicago area. *Photo courtesy of the La Porte County Historical Society.*

By the end of the century, the Sorensons were living in their last home together, at 621 Alma Street in Austin, a handsome two-story with a pretty porch and a large yard. Mads was a good husband to Bella and was genuinely in love with her and his family, but he was finally developing a true understanding of his wife. He knew now that no matter how much he gave her—and he was very generous—Bella still wanted more. He also began to believe that she didn't love him, indeed maybe didn't even care for him and likely never had. He too, as clueless as he was because he was constantly working, began to wonder about the missing children. But then he would remind himself, she was his wife, and he owed her loyalty. He was a good Norwegian husband, and he would take care of his family and not let suspicions crowd his brain.

Bella confided to her sister that she wouldn't have stayed with Mads if he didn't make a decent living. Nellie, who couldn't understand her sister, became upset and rose to Mads's defense. But the sister she knew, the farm girl who scavenged for snurkvist, had become a stranger, a high-living, demanding woman who saw money as her only goal, her only pleasure.

Around ten o'clock on the morning of July 30, 1900, Jennie's friends from the neighborhood, Cora and Harriet, stopped by to ask if she wanted to pick apples with them. Relieved to see that Bella wasn't outside, they waved at Mads, who was sitting on the front porch bouncing Myrtle and Lucy on his knee. Like many of the other children who came to live in the Sorenson home, the two little girls had just suddenly appeared, and like all of the children, they were very pretty. But unlike most of the young children who were seen playing in the large yard or running through the house, Myrtle and Lucy hadn't yet disappeared.

Cora and Harriet expected that Bella would tell Jennie she couldn't go with them to pick apples. Typically, Bella made Jennie stay inside when the girls stopped by to invite her to play. Sometimes she might let Jennie visit with the two on the front porch, but she too would sit with them, listening in on their conversations and criticizing what the girls said. But today was different. Jennie came out, happy to say that she could go apple picking. She was so excited about the excursion she laughingly gave Mads a kiss and skipped down the steps. Both the girls and Mads were surprised but were quick to take advantage of Jennie's sudden freedom. Mads, smiling, gave them money for ice cream and waved them off on their journey, and the girls left for Ridgeland to gather apples before Bella could change her mind.

Bella took care of Lucy and Myrtle as Mads ate the lunch she had made for him. He'd been fine, but suddenly now his head began to throb, and he told Bella he was going upstairs to sleep. Bella fussed over him, insisting he take the medicinal powder she added to a glass of water. Not one to say no to Bella, as it caused her to be very angry—not a pleasant thing for those around her—Mads took the medication. Still fully clothed, he lay down atop the bed's covers. He never woke up.

What happened isn't clear. One neighbor said she heard Mads say, "Bella, you poisoned me," and then a cry of immense pain from Mads before Bella abruptly shut the door. Bella had, as one would expect, a different story. She'd returned to check on Mads and, finding him unresponsive, sent for Dr. J. B. Miller, who had boarded with them for a while. Miller, seeing Mads's lifeless body arched in an unnatural position with one hand gripping the bed frame tightly, immediately recognized the symptoms of strychnine poisoning. What happened, he asked, and Bella told him she'd given Mads quinine powder because of his headache. Believing the druggist had inadvertently given Bella strychnine instead of quinine, Miller told Bella to fetch the paper it came in. She couldn't, she said; she'd burned it after administering the medicine. That seemed odd, thought Miller, as Bella had told him that Mads started crying out in pain as soon as he took the medicine. How had she had time to burn the paper, and why would she do such a thing when her husband was in extreme pain?

Wanting to confirm the cause of Mads's death, Miller told Bella he was going to perform an autopsy. Bella became hysterical, moaning and sobbing. She couldn't bear the thought of her beloved husband being cut open and defiled in such a manner. She started wailing at the top of her lungs and insisted on summoning their family physician, Dr. Charles E. Jones, who, when he arrived, tried his best to comfort the grieving and distraught new widow. Anxious to quiet her as her lamentations were getting louder and louder, Jones told Miller he'd been treating Mads for an enlarged heart and he was sure heart failure was the cause of Mads's death. Not wanting to challenge the older and more experienced doctor, Miller reluctantly agreed to sign the death certificate.

Jennie and her friends returned around five o'clock that afternoon, carrying baskets of apples and talking of making pies and tarts and maybe even an apple cake. She had promised Cora and Harriet some lemonade but stopped short on the porch steps, sensing a change in the atmosphere. Neighbors were standing around looking at the house but didn't approach the girls. It was all so quiet, almost creepy, and when Jennie went inside, she found Bella sitting at the kitchen table intently adding up numbers. The floorboard creaked beneath Jennie's footsteps, and Bella looked up.

Your papa is dead, Bella said matter-of-factly, no longer the grieving widow but instead all business and no emotion. You'll need to start doing more around the house now and take care of Myrtle and Lucy. I'll have other things to do to keep this household going.

Jennie, disbelieving, stared at Bella. Before the tears could come, she ran back outside. She cried in the embraces of her friends, and they in turn cooed softly, trying to calm her.

Neighbors also coddled Jennie, but when they stepped away, Jennie could overhear the low murmur of whispered questions and accusations as they talked. When Bella stepped out onto the porch, her silhouette creating a dark shadow against the doorframe, she stood silent while she eyed the gathering of friends and neighbors, people who had come to offer solace, women who would help prepare the body, and men who would make the coffin. Judging the mood of the crowd, Bella began to cry, sobbing Mads's name, and called Jennie to her.

We will go in and grieve as a family, she addressed the crowd. Thank you for coming.

As she started back into the house, she saw Cora and Harriet were following, still holding Jennie's hands. She turned to them and bent very low, so her face was close to theirs, and she hissed, This is a family matter, not some type of social call. Now go home.

Harriet, who was full of courage because of her desire to help her friend, said, Jennie needs us.

Go home, I said, whispered Bella, her voice threatening. The look on her face was terrifying. The girls dropped Jennie's hands and walked down the stairs, leaving their friend alone with a woman they believed had killed her adopted father. Bella straightened up, her face now full of grief, and called out to Harriet and Cora, Thank you, sweethearts, for being such good friends to Jennie. The two girls looked at each other and hurried on. As much as they loved Jennie, they were glad to be away from her mother.

Mads's brothers had long suspected Bella of trying to kill their brother after he once collapsed while eating a dinner she'd cooked for him. At the time, the doctors thought he would die, but he had somehow managed to pull through. The brothers remained convinced that she had poisoned his food and told Mads so. As for Mads, well, he loved his wife and laughed at his brothers' warnings.

The Sorenson brothers had expected this would happen again, and they were sure they were right when they heard about Mads's cries, the neighbors' accusations against Bella, and the burned medicine packaging. They talked to the pharmacist, and he insisted he gave Bella quinine. The poison was kept separate in another area. There was no way it could have been a mistake. Mads's brothers became even more convinced it was murder when they found out about the double insurance payments Bella stood to gain for Mads's death.

It couldn't be coincidence, they thought, that Mads's new insurance policy started on July 30, 1900, while his old one was still active, overlapping by just one day. Since the doctors said Mads had died of a heart condition, Bella collected a total of $8,500 (roughly a quarter-million dollars today).

Mads's brother Oscar made the trip to Chicago to ensure his brother received justice. Oscar collected the testimony of a neighbor who stated she had seen Mads on that day and he was in good health and of usual vigor, and she saw Bella give Mads a glass from which he drank right before he became ill. Oscar insisted on an autopsy and convinced the authorities to order an inquest. Mads's body was exhumed, much to Bella's dismay.

Two doctors performed the autopsy after consulting the death certificate, which read, "enlargement of the heart." The heart was indeed enlarged, and therefore, the doctors felt there was no need to go any further. Oscar demanded the stomach contents be examined, reiterating his belief that Mads had been poisoned. They agreed to test for poison, but Oscar would have to pay the large fee. He didn't have the money, neither did his brothers. As far as the authorities were concerned, the doctors' findings proved the cause of death matched the death certificate. Oscar could do little but watch as his brother was buried again, ashamed he hadn't given him the justice he deserved.

Before he left though, Oscar relayed his story and suspicions to all who would listen. And there were plenty of ears. The neighbors had already suspected Bella of partaking in the baby-farming business; they bore witness to the several fires that allowed the Sorenson family to move each time to a better home; and they had all heard the whispers of Caroline and Axel dying under suspicious circumstances and the profit Bella gained from their deaths. They also shared stories of the other children who came to live with Bella and then vanished. Could murdering her husband really be too much of a stretch?

When Bella heard the rumors, she knew it was time to move on.

3

A New Home and a New Husband

BELLA HAD COME SO FAR—FROM ABJECT POVERTY IN RURAL Norway to prosperity in one of America's most exciting cities. But with Mads dead and double the insurance money in hand, she was on the move again. For some reason, Bella, who had toiled on hardscrabble farms in Norway and journeyed over four thousand miles across the ocean to get away from those potato fields and cows, decided to buy a forty-three-acre farm about a mile outside of La Porte, Indiana.

At one time, this region of lakes, forests, and prairies was part of the great Potawatomi Nation. French explorers who navigated Lake Michigan by canoe and were known as voyageurs called the area *descheim*, French for "by the lakes." The opening from the great forests onto the lush prairie was termed *la porte*, French for "passageway." La Porte became a county in 1832, and in 1852, the city of La Porte was incorporated. The La Porte Medical School—the first of its kind in the Midwest—opened in 1842. By then, land belonging to the peaceful Potawatomi had been confiscated and the tribe forced on a deadly march known as the Trail of Death from Indiana to Kansas. Prosperous, La Porte was the county seat but second in size to Michigan City, the county's largest city and a busy port on Lake Michigan.

Bella's La Porte was a lovely little lakeside town with a population of about ten thousand in 1900, conveniently connected to

The Marian Ridgeway polygonal barn shown here was built in 1878 and would have been a familiar site to Belle. The barn, which is still standing, is located on US 35. *Photo courtesy of Library of Congress.*

Chicago by train and to many other communities by interurbans. At the thriving downtown's center sat a magnificent three-story red-sandstone courthouse embellished with a tower, gargoyles, and stained-glass windows; it is still there today. Boulevards such as Indiana and Michigan Avenues boasted tree-lined streets and lush lawns fronting stately mansions.

Opulence extended to the four mansions built by one of the town's founders, John Walker, for his children. One in particular, located among the fertile farmland surrounding La Porte, harbored a past worthy of Bella.

Built in 1846 by Walker for his daughter Harriet Holcomb and her husband, the large two-story, six-bedroom brick home was just a mile north of La Porte on McClung Road, close enough to be convenient to town, far enough away for assured privacy. The property also housed a barn and stable, had acres of orchards and fertile fields, and abutted a small lake.

The Holcombs were Confederate sympathizers, and La Porte was solidly Union territory. In fact, according to Jason Packard, brigadier general during the Civil War, "few counties in the state of Indiana manifested a greater devotion to the country" than did La

The historic La Porte County Courthouse. *Photo courtesy of Library of Congress.*

Porte County during the Civil War. The county had three Civil War camps, regiments camps on the county fairgrounds, and two hospitals for soldiers. The county also sent 2,750 men to serve the Union and suffered losses of approximately 10 percent. In other words, La Porte had no tolerance for Confederate sympathies, founding family or no. The Holcombs got the message, abandoned the house, and moved to New York.

The home would have thirteen owners, several of whom met unfortunate ends, before Bella moved in. Two brothers suddenly and mysteriously died at the same time. A woman sick with grief over a love affair poisoned herself. And a man hanged himself from his bedpost and lingered thereafter to haunt the stairway.

But death wasn't the only legacy this house left. In 1892, Mattie Altic, a flamboyant madam from Chicago, closed her business in the city and moved out to the farm, bringing high living, along with the women who worked for her, to the small, quiet town. She quickly added a jetty, boathouse, and expansive carriage house. She installed a marble bar in her parlor and decorated the main house with a flourish only a demimondaine could pull off. The townsfolk,

Downtown La Porte scene around the turn of the century.
Photo courtesy of Library of Congress.

horrified and curious, tried to glimpse the clients being picked up at the train station even though curtains covered the windows of the surrey.

Mattie dressed the part of a working gal from Chicago's vice-riddled Levee, her clothing ostentatious and her large hats embellished with enormous ostrich plumes. Decades later, those who had encountered her and the women who worked for her still marveled at the sight of these wonders.

Mattie and her entourage would go for jaunts in a fringed surrey pulled by beautiful and expensive or "fancy" horses, as they were described by townspeople. White reins guided the horses, no brown chapped leather for these horses and these women. All was extravagant and designed to make a great show. When Mattie and her women flounced into a store—their perfume sweet and thick, their makeup shocking—the clerks and owners fawned over them, catering to their needs and charging prices far higher than the typical La Porte lady would ever think of paying. Mattie, with a flourish, would pull out her pocketbook and pile bills on the counter. Her driver would carry the wonderfully wrapped boxes to the surrey. Once home, the horses would be groomed and then housed in equally fancy stables.

As for Mattie's famous ostrich plumes, one young boy who visited her home with his uncle, a veterinarian called upon to treat the horses, could still recall their magnificence eighty years later—they were the largest he'd ever seen.

Mattie was not a woman who had moved to the country for solitude. Indeed, she became well known for her raucous parties drawing many of her Chicago cohorts. Her good friends Aldermen "Hinky Dink" Michael Kenna and "Bathhouse" John Coughlin were Chicago politicians so corrupt that their ill-repute is still known today. The two lived and worked in Chicago's notorious Levee District. Known for its booze, white slavery, prostitution, lasciviousness, knifings, and murders, the Levee was a wild place where Hinky Dink and Bathhouse were the law and ran a protection action, shaking down local businessmen for 10 percent of their profits. There was a whole lot of shaking to do as the Levee was a cesspool of vice; its businesses included gambling houses, dance halls, saloons, and brothels where every type of sexual whim could be fulfilled, including, for those interested, torture rooms and lascivious live sex acts. In other words, 10 percent of all that was no small amount.

Many of Mattie's girls delighted in the carriage rides, the rowboat rides on Fish Lake, and the gawking looks given them by handsome farm boys who had never seen painted ladies before. Mattie was careful to hide the iron bars on the windows with a fancy facade. But there was little doubt Mattie brought the vice of Chicago and the ugliness of white slavery to La Porte.

It all came to an end one night, when Mattie supposedly died of a heart attack after a long evening of hard partying. Believable as that is, it's but one version of her demise. Another story relates the sad tale that she committed suicide after being jilted by a lover. Yet another cries sororicide. Mattie had taken her sister, Eva Ruppert, who ran a competing brothel in South Bend, to court claiming Eva was trying to poison her. Many believe Eva finally succeeded. If so, it was most likely the first of many murders, but not unexplained and odd deaths, to occur on the property.

The house Bella chose, given its history, had a dark aura, though she would be the one to inspire others to call it evil.

In November 1901, a large Norwegian woman with a thick accent pulled $13,000 ($368,281) in cash out of a cloth satchel to pay for the home. Bella was back on the farm. She immediately insured the carriage house and the boat pavilion, two buildings she had very little use for (and which burned down shortly thereafter), and moved in with her three children, Jennie, Myrtle, and Lucy. She changed her name slightly with this new start. La Porte would know her as Belle.

Now that she had a new farm and a new name, Belle needed a new man. She took part in the common practice of her fellow immigrants of the day and advertised in a variety of Scandinavian papers.

Peter Frederickson of Janesville, Wisconsin, answered Belle's matrimonial advertisement, so Belle traveled to Janesville to investigate the situation. She was pleased to discover Frederickson's home, free of liens, was valued at $1,500 and he had $1,000 in life insurance. While Belle was used to greater sums, she found the investment satisfactory, and the wedding was set. But Belle had another stipulation. She didn't want to live in Janesville, a pleasant city just across the state line from Illinois and a little over one hundred miles from Chicago. She asked Frederickson to sell his house and move in with her.

Frederickson agreed, but his Norwegian housekeeper, Mrs. Gunness, cautioned him not to marry "that woman." Maybe she had heard the rumors about Mads's death or even about the boy back in Selbu. Her warnings went unheeded. Frederickson went ahead and arranged a wedding supper, but after his friends refused to attend, he became convinced it wasn't such a good idea to marry the widow and ended the engagement.

Belle was livid. She blamed Mrs. Gunness for ruining her plans. Belle had a penchant for revenge, and her next choice of husband may have been more than just chance. Mrs. Gunness had a recently widowed son by the name of Peder, who was called Peter, the Americanized version of the name. Coincidentally, Belle first met Peter Gunness in 1893 in Chicago, the same year as the World's Fair. Born in 1872, Peter, like Mads and Belle, was a Norwegian emigrant, arriving from Sandsvær, Buskerud, Norway. He'd moved to Chicago to work in the stockyards, where he rented a room from the Sorensons. Peter was a handsome, well-built man with bright blue eyes—a true Viking type—and one who easily caught the eye of the ladies in the community, Belle included.

Peter Gunness's gravestone. *Photo courtesy of Dale Hop.*

Peter's time with the Sorensons was short-lived, however, and he ended up moving closer to family. He married Janna Sofie "Jennie Sophia" Simonsdatter, who was eight years his senior. The couple's first child, Swanhild Christine Gunness, was born on January 25, 1897. A second child named Lydia was born on October 31, 1899, and died the following August. Jennie Gunness gave birth to their third child, also named Jennie, on September 1, 1901. But while the baby survived, her mother did not. She died that same day, leaving Peter with a baby and a young daughter to raise on his own. Widowed men with children married quickly, creating an ideal opportunity for Belle. She didn't waste time. Seven months to the day of Jennie's death, on April 1, 1902, Belle married Peter Gunness at the First Baptist Church of La Porte.

A few days after Peter and his two children moved into the La Porte farmhouse, Dr. Martin, a local physician, was called to attend seven-month-old Jennie Gunness. Though Belle told him upon his arrival that the little girl was seriously ill, the doctor couldn't find any signs that the baby was sick and left. Two days later, the doctor was called again, but this time, little Jennie, who was home alone with her new stepmother, was dead.

Though Martin believed the babe had been smothered, there was no proof, and the official cause of death was listed as edema of the lungs. Before the end of the year, little Jennie's father would be dead as well.

Around 3:00 a.m. on Tuesday, December 16, the Nicholson family was awakened by a loud banging on their door. Standing outside in the cold was twelve-year-old Jennie Olsen.

"Mama wants you to come up," she said. "Papa's burned himself."

When Swan Nicholson and his son Albert entered the Gunness home just a few minutes later, a motionless Peter was lying face down on the parlor floor and a hysterical Belle was sitting in the kitchen. Swan felt for a pulse but found none. He told his son to get the doctor, and Albert ran all the way to town to where Dr. Bo Bowell lived.

Together they rode back to the house in the doctor's buggy. When Bowell examined Peter's body, he saw the back of his head was bloody and his nose was broken and bent to one side. He was not only dead, but rigor mortis had already set in, a sign he had been dead longer than Belle said.

The doctor, who also served as the coroner for La Porte County, believed Peter had been murdered. He had questions for the new widow, but she was too hysterical to tell a coherent story about what had happened. Finally, between the sobbing and the wailing—the same outpouring of emotion she'd shown when Mads died—the doctor and the Nicholsons were able to gather that Peter went into the kitchen to lock the doors and get his shoes, which he kept by the stove to keep warm. When he bent over to retrieve the shoes, a meat grinder poised on the shelf above him fell on the back of his head and a hot container of brine that Belle was heating up on the stove overturned and spilled, scalding his neck.

After this series of accidents occurred, Belle applied some baking soda to Peter's neck to avoid blistering and then rubbed the burn further with Vaseline and liniment. She didn't notice the broken nose, but she saw the cut on his head. Peter complained only about the burn, so Belle thought little of the cut.

After a while, she told them between sobs, Peter said he was feeling better, so Belle fixed up the lounge in the parlor for him, as it was warmer than upstairs. She then climbed the steps alone to their bedroom.

A La Porte gas station around the time Belle lived there. *Photo courtesy of Library of Congress.*

She was sleeping when she heard Peter calling her name, and she came running down the stairs to discover Peter lying on the parlor floor, holding his head and moaning as if in pain. Calling to Jennie, she told the girl to dress quickly and get help at the Nicholsons, their nearest neighbors.

As Belle told her story, the two men and young Albert believed she was lying. The story just didn't fit together. But no one said a word. After watching the doctor drive away down the dark road back to town, Albert shared his suspicions that Peter had been murdered. Swan, not wanting trouble, particularly from Belle, who when angry would shoot over the heads of neighbors, told his son to keep it to himself. They didn't want to cause trouble, he said. Bowell too was suspicious and conducted the postmortem that very afternoon along with Dr. Martin, the doctor who had been suspicious of Jennie's death.

The autopsy showed Peter's nose was broken and his head had sustained deep lacerations, the most serious of which was one inch long and so deep it cut through the scalp and the external layer of the skull, resulting in an intercranial hemorrhage—the ultimate cause of death. Bowell and Martin could find no trace of the burns

Belle said were caused by the hot brine. The discrepancies between Belle's story and Peter's injuries were indeed suspicious.

The inquest was held two days later, and Belle, true to form, wailed and carried on about her dead husband. She told the same story as she had the evening Peter died. For those who didn't know better, it was easy to believe that she was a widow so overcome with grief that she couldn't even testify in a comprehensible way.

Swan Nicholson, called as a witness, said no, he didn't think Peter had been murdered.

Jennie also was questioned. She repeated almost verbatim the same story her mother had told. Bowell, pretty sure that Jennie was lying, asked her about the death of Mads Sorenson and whether he had been insured—hoping to show that dead husbands and insurance payments were nothing new for Belle. It was a good try, but Belle played a better hand. When he asked the questions, she cranked up the hysterics to a new high. Bowell was stuck. All three witnesses said it was an accident, and there was no other proof except the inconsistencies between Belle's story and the facts.

The inquest did not call on Myrtle to testify, though if it had, it might have heard the same accusation Myrtle whispered to a classmate years later: "My mama killed my papa. She hit him with a meat cleaver and he died. Don't tell a soul."

Bowell was forced to rule Peter's death as an accident. Once again, Belle got away with murder.

Peter was buried three days later. Belle was too busy to attend some of the proceedings before her husband's internment, according to Charles Way, a pallbearer at Peter's funeral. She instead was in La Porte consulting with an attorney regarding her possible arrest for killing her husband. But she did find time to file a death claim with the insurance company—for which she collected money.

Belle failed to tell Peter's family he was dead. It took three weeks for the news to reach them. Soon after, Peter's brother Gustav arrived from Wisconsin wanting to know what happened. He hadn't spent long at the farm before his suspicions made him determined to meet with Sheriff Albert Smutzer and demand an investigation.

The sheriff stated that an inquest had already been held and the case was closed. Smutzer's refusal to investigate further wasn't a surprise to those who knew the sheriff. After all, they'd say to each other, wasn't his fancy red roadster often parked in front of the widow's house?

Returning to the farm, Gustav demanded Belle turn over Peter's estate to Swanhild, his remaining child. Unfortunately, Belle said, Peter cashed out the policy to buy stocks in a mine, but if it ever panned out, Swanhild would be rich. When Gustav asked to see the stock certificates, Belle couldn't locate them.

Gustav was sure that not only had Belle murdered his niece and his brother but that Swanhild, if she stayed in the home, would be in grave danger as well. He told Belle he was going to take Swanhild back to Wisconsin so she could live with Peter's family, but Belle refused to let her go. Instead, she said, Gustav should come live with her and manage the farm.

Not long after, Belle awoke in the middle of the night. She wasn't sure what had woken her. Maybe she had heard a door softly being closed or a creak on the stairs as someone lightly tiptoed down. She wasn't sure, but she felt a sudden surge of anger and fear. She rushed to where Swanhild slept. The bed was empty. She hurried down to the guest room and silently turned the knob. Gustav had been keeping it locked at night after he retired for the night. She knew this because several times she had tried to enter his room when she thought he might be sleeping. This time, it turned easily in her hand, and as the door swung open, she knew what she was going to see—another empty bed. They must have just left, she thought, hurrying downstairs. It wasn't safe to let them go— Swanhild had seen so much, and she might, when she was older, understand what she had seen. Or she might talk too much, and others might be able to piece things together. Also, there went an inheritance she would have gotten if Swanhild had happened to die while living with her.

When Belle reached the front door, she saw the bolts were thrown back. They certainly had gone out this way. She opened the door and looked out. Moonlight flooded the dirt road that ran past the house. There was no one on the road. Either they were going through the fields or were too far ahead on the road, or maybe they had run over to a neighbor's house. Even if she got dressed and hitched up the buggy, what could she do if she caught up with them? There was no way to really make them come back unless she pulled the shotgun on them. If Swanhild said anything, she would just say it was the imagination of a silly little girl. She had lied her way out of more difficult situations; she could do so again.

While she stood on the porch, pondering her options, Gustav and Swanhild were running through the fields toward the railroad tracks not far from Belle's, where they would try to flag the train down. Gustav raised the lantern he had taken from the house as soon as he heard the sound of the engine. An immense sense of relief came over him when the sound of the brakes being applied carried through the still night air. They had timed it perfectly, he thought with relief. Beside him, he heard Swanhild stifle a sob. The poor girl had been so afraid and so brave when he told her of the plan. Now, he thought as they boarded the steps up into the first passenger car, Swanhild could live a normal life in safety. He hadn't been able to avenge his brother's death, but he could save Swanhild. It was the least he could do for his brother. They both settled into their seats, watching the dark scenery flash by.

Soon Swanhild was asleep with her head on his shoulder. He looked down at her sweet face, her dark lashes touching smooth creamy cheeks, her small arms tight around a stuffed bear that was a long-ago present from her father. Gustav was fearful at the first few stops, expecting Belle to step aboard. Only when the train rounded north, following the curve of Lake Michigan as it traveled through Chicago to Wisconsin, did he allow himself to sleep a little. When they pulled into the station nearest the farm and he saw his brothers waiting for him, he realized he'd never been so happy to see them. They were safe, thought Gustav. They had outwitted her.

But the danger wasn't really over. The family soon started seeing a strange man hanging around. They were sure he was spying on them and came to believe that he was planning to kidnap Swanhild at Belle's behest. So she was sent to live with a wealthy man the family knew well. There, they believed, she would be safe.

Talking to a reporter, Swanhild recalled her days in La Porte with Belle:

> She was a mean woman, and I was always afraid of her, but she never treated me bad while Papa was there, only she scolded me

and sometimes she slapped me. I was never happy all that time I was there, and I was always afraid of that woman. I was afraid of Jennie Olsen. Once I tried to go down in the cellar and she ran after me and looked so mean when she shook me that I was afraid to go there again. So were Myrtle and Lucy. I don't know why she did not want us to go there, but Myrtle and Lucy said we must never dare to. Jennie Olsen was afraid to go in the cellar too. Sometimes Mrs. Gunness would send us out of the house to play but her children didn't like me and so I would play with Sport. Sport is the nicest dog. He would run after sticks and he loved me all the time.

I never could call Mrs. Gunness momma. She never seemed like a real mama. Sometimes she would send us to our rooms and lock us in. Then we would hear her talking to someone. She never let us go in the kitchen either. Myrtle and Lucy were tattletales. After Papa was gone, they would go to their momma and tell her that I was kicking on the wall when she locked us in. I wasn't really but she whipped me awful.

She treated me all right when Papa was around, but all of us were afraid of her, even Myrtle and Lucy, her own two little girls, and Jennie Olsen was, too. After Papa died, she treated us even worse than ever.

Pretty soon after Papa died that woman began having men come to see her again. I stayed there almost a year after my papa died. I was afraid of Mrs. Gunness all the time and was glad when Uncle Gust came and got me, and I came away to Janesville where my grandma lived.

Swanhild was kept safe, and she was never bothered by Belle again. But even so, the girl remained fearful well into her adulthood, even after she married and had children of her own. Indeed, her son remembered her as afraid until she died an elderly woman.

Belle, for her part, seemed to move quickly from an inconsolable widow to a woman secure in her innocence of murder.

Mrs. George Olander, Jennie Olsen's older sister, lived in Chicago and read about the death of Peter Gunness in the newspaper. Surprised that Belle hadn't notified the family, she decided to pay a visit to offer her sympathies. For the first half hour, Belle didn't mention her husband's recent death. When Olander brought it up, Belle asked her how she knew about the accident. Olander explained it was in the paper.

Belle laughed a little, marveling that the news had reached Chicago, and then said she wasn't in need of consolation.

Swanhild Gunness; her husband, Harry Reuterskiold; with their son, Vernon. *Photo courtesy of Vernon Reuterskiold.*

How did Peter die? Olander asked.

Belle replied he'd gone to town to buy a meat grinder and when reaching for one on an upper shelf, it had fallen on his head, killing him. That was, of course, not at all what happened or what Olander had read in the newspaper. But this was typical of the games Belle played. She knew Olander knew differently and was challenging her to see if Olander would contradict her new version of the event. But Olander didn't—just like so many others. Belle was beyond caring about what Jennie's sister thought. Peter was cold in the ground, and she had been cleared of any wrongdoing.

Though it would take years to put all the clues together, there were other oddities going on at the farm, and people were noticing. Charles F. Pahrman, a young man who worked as a clerk in a local hardware store, had helped Belle with some of the carpentry work when she first moved into the six-bedroom house. He helped open the drain spouts, fixed the shutters, and helped reinforce the old barn. But he was baffled by another chore he was asked to do. Belle hired him to build a pigpen with a fence that was six feet high and topped with barbed wire. What pig could jump half that height, he wondered.

There was another incident that was whispered about. A peddler pulled up to Belle's house and went inside to show off his wares. He never returned, and his horse and buggy sat there through the day until Belle took them into her stable. Later, she was seen driving that buggy around. People talked, but she didn't care.

As time went on, she started feeling all-powerful and untouchable. Though the man she sent to kidnap Swanhild had reported back that she had disappeared, it had been quite a while since they'd left, so whatever the child might be saying, no one seemed to be acting on it. Besides, she was sure Smutzer wouldn't investigate any story anyone brought to him. It would end in his office like it always did. Just like before, she had gotten away with it. Belle had been getting away with so much for so long, she believed she could outsmart anyone, and time after time she was proven right. It was time to get on with her plans.

Now that Peter was dead, Belle started advertising again:

Personal — comely widow who owns a large farm in one of the finest districts in La Porte County, Indiana, desires to make the acquaintance of gentleman equally well provided, with view of joining fortunes. No replies by letter considered unless sender is willing to follow answer with personal visit. Triflers need not apply.

4

Disappearing Farmhands and Suitors

BELLE HAD DAYDREAMED OF A LIFE OF LEISURE WHILE TEND-ing cows in the vast fields of Norway. But somewhere along the way, those girlish fantasies turned into an obsession. Though she was now quite well off, with three beautiful, well-behaved children—though that may have been due to fear of her heavy hand—and a grand home, it wasn't enough. This all-consuming need for more led to days filled with farm chores and frequent trips to the post office and evenings spent writing letters and concocting mysterious plots.

Cursing, Belle once again found herself doing the chores required of a farm now that Peter was gone. Of course, Jennie helped with the farm work and took care of Myrtle and Lucy, but Belle still had her own share to do. She milked the cows, tended to the live-stock, pitched hay, plowed the land, and planted and harvested the crop. Belle was often spotted at auctions and in the fields tromping around in muck boots and overalls. Tall and strong, she was just as capable as any man, had the strength to meet any challenge, and, some said, looked like a man in that garb.

The farmers' wives were also struck by Belle's fortitude—at least those who believed she gave birth all on her own shortly after Peter's death.

"Mother has gotten a little baby boy," said Jennie Olsen excit-edly, standing in the doorway of the Lapham home, announcing the arrival of Philip Gunness. Wanting to help, Mrs. Catherine Lapham went over to the Gunness farm expecting to see Belle in bed recuperating. Instead, she found her standing outside by the cistern at the back door, washing the baby's cloths.

"You shouldn't be up," said Catherine.

"In the old country, they never go to bed after getting a baby," Belle replied.

Catherine wasn't the only one surprised by the forty-three-year-old new mother's resiliency. When the midwife showed at the scheduled time to help with the delivery, she found Philip to be birthed, bathed, and dressed. Mrs. Swan Nicholson, who also had promised to be there for the lying-in, wasn't allowed in the house when she showed up at the expected time. Mrs. Louisa Diesslin, calling at the farm the day after the baby was born, found Belle in the yard chasing pigs. She went upstairs and found Philip lying on a large bed by himself.

All the neighbors agreed Philip looked older than a newborn. One neighbor whispered that the night before Philip's birth, a woman arrived at the Gunness farm with a baby but left alone. Adding to the mystery, Belle did not register Philip's birth with the county or the state. And Peter's family didn't try to obtain custody like they did with Swanhild.

Talk and suspicion among the community was once again swirling around Belle. No one could quite make out her character. She was a loving and doting mother, and the girls always seemed so happy. They wore the best clothes and went to Sunday school every week. Belle even visited neighbor children when they were sick. However, she was very strict about boundaries. She had several rows with neighbors over livestock roaming past their borders, and she once chased some children who were digging for sassafras roots off with a baseball bat because they were too close to her fence line. A couple of times, she pulled her shotgun on a neighbor for some issue or another.

Even with Belle's independence and resourcefulness, the farm was just too much for one person to operate, so she hired a farmhand. Roughly thirty years old and handsome, Olaf Lindboe had immigrated to Chicago from Norway three years earlier. He answered Belle's ad for a hired hand in the *Skandinaven* and moved to La Porte with his life savings of $600.

Olaf quickly settled into his room in the house and made friends with the neighbors. He and Belle found a rhythm, often working side by side. Belle enjoyed his company and was kind to him. Neighbors began to notice and comment on how close they had become.

Belle's attentions, including her trips to his bedroom late at night, led him to believe that she favored him as a suitor, and after just a couple of months, he told his father he would be getting married soon. This confidence extended to his position on the farm—not as a hired hand, but as the master.

One night after dinner, he was playing a game with the children when Lucy put her arm around his neck and said, I love you.

I love all of you, Olaf returned, and the girls all giggled and threw their arms around his neck. A loud noise came from the kitchen. They all turned to find Belle standing in the doorway. She gave them all a cold look and then went back into the kitchen. They heard a cabinet door slam shut.

Belle didn't come to his bed that night, and in the morning, she was cold to him as he ate a quick breakfast. He tried to start a conversation about the farm, suggesting they rotate the crops the next season. She turned her back to him, and when he went to kiss her goodbye, she pulled away.

Jealous of the children's affection and infuriated by Olaf's assumptions about his role on the farm, Belle fell into a dark mood. Olaf was soon gone.

His sudden disappearance raised eyebrows. He was a friendly sort and not one to leave without saying goodbye to his friends.

One of the neighbors, Chris Christofferson, came upon Belle plowing the cornfield, which would have been Olaf's job. When Chris inquired, Belle, rather irritated, said he'd left her in the middle of the season knowing full well the plowing needed to be done. He had gone off to St. Louis, she said, to see the World's Fair and buy some land there. Chris thought back to the last time he had seen Olaf. The farmhand had been moving the privy, and he hadn't mentioned a word about St. Louis.

Swan Nicholson received a different answer from Belle about Olaf's disappearance: he'd returned to Norway for the crowning of the new king.

Olaf's father, who hadn't heard from his son in months, wrote to Belle inquiring about his son's whereabouts. He received a short reply: Olaf had moved out west to set up a homestead. She didn't know where.

A few months later, she hired another farmhand, Henry Gurholt. Much like Olaf, Henry was happy with his new accommodations and quickly settled into the community, turning neighbors into friends with his pleasant disposition.

Belle was kind and made him feel like part of the family. Henry told his mother as much when he wrote to her shortly after his arrival. He also commented on the beauty of the home and property.

By all accounts, Henry seemed pleased with his situation, so it was surprising that he too abruptly disappeared during harvest-time. Again, Belle was left without help in the middle of a major task. She asked Chris to help her finish the work. She was less than forthcoming with information when he asked after the second missing farmhand. Henry, she said, had taken ill and left suddenly for Chicago—so suddenly in fact that he took only one satchel of clothes, leaving behind the rest of his belongings.

Chris found it even more suspicious that winter when he saw Belle wearing Henry's heavy fur coat. If he went to Chicago, why didn't he take his coat, Chris asked. Belle's brief reply was that Henry never wrote asking her to send his belongings. She hadn't heard from him at all, in fact.

Belle hired several farmhands over the next few years. She asked that they perform odd jobs in addition to the typical farm work. For instance, Belle couldn't stand to hurt an animal and often asked the farmhands to chop off the head of the chicken for Sunday dinner. She also had them dig large pits throughout her property. For trash, she said. These men too left without a word to neighbors and friends, and Belle constantly complained about how difficult it was to keep help.

Hired hands, while necessary for her farm and as lovers, were not an investment she cared to cultivate. More important matters required her attention. Belle continued her search for a husband, posting advertisements such as the following.

WANTED—A woman who owns a beautifully located and valuable farm in first class condition, wants a good and reliable man as partner in same. Some little cash is required and will be furnished first class security.

She used a variety of names including Mrs. Jennie Hinckley, Mrs. Belle Sorenson, Marga Olsen, and Miss Jennie Sorenson, the latter the name of both Peter's first wife and his daughter. Belle had a black sense of humor.

Even with a new baby to care for, Belle continued her search for men and money. In addition to receiving letters at the La Porte post office, she most likely had an agent who was collecting letters for her at post offices in Chicago; Peru, Indiana; and Champaign, Illinois; and she may have taken it a step further and run her own matrimonial agency in Warsaw, Indiana. Her agent may have been a young man named Julius G. Truelson, who had met her through one of her ads. He had no money but was willing to help her in her endeavors on and off in the years to come.

The numerous names and post offices were likely to keep others from discovering what she was up to. This was no small feat. Such schemes could have only been maintained by the most organized of minds. Not only did she have to keep the names and stories straight, she also had to ensure that suitors did not visit at the same time.

With her correspondence, Belle quickly sorted the wheat from the chaff, writing in Norwegian in a very direct manner, outlining the requirements necessary for would-be suitors, which included at least $1,000 security. She was not the type of woman to waste time. She wanted men with money, and she wasn't shy about letting them know it. Surprisingly this tactic worked, and Belle often received between four and ten letters a day.

Belle's strategy was to pique men's interest with her advertisement of matrimony and wealth, charm them with a series of love letters that also highlighted her cooking skills and hinted at conjugal bliss, implore them to keep their relationship a secret, and insist they cash out their assets and come to La Porte to prove their worth.

Neighbors would often see Belle, with her hair up and in fashionable clothes, riding alongside men in her carriage on Sunday afternoons. Sometimes Belle introduced the men as her cousins, sometimes as fiancés. She was a different woman when suitors were around, girlish in her coquettishness, womanly in her allure.

One such suitor was George Anderson. Thirty-nine-year-old George of Tarkio, Missouri, responded to one of Belle's advertisements. After an exchange of letters, Belle invited him to La Porte, where they were to be married. Bringing only $300 with him, George arrived to check out Belle's farm for himself before committing to marriage. Belle was disappointed to learn he hadn't sold his property before arriving.

That evening at dinner, George tried to engage little Myrtle, but the child, pale and quiet, just stared at him with wide eyes. After dinner, he was shown to his bedroom on the second floor and quickly fell asleep.

George awoke suddenly with the feeling of being watched. He found Belle leaning over him. Startled, he yelled. Belle, surprised, jumped back and fled the room.

Feeling he was in danger, George dressed quickly and left the farmhouse without a word, running along the road toward La Porte. He waited for hours at the train station before finally boarding a train to Missouri. He never spoke to Belle again, not even to retrieve the belongings he hastily left behind.

Not all suitors made it back home. An elderly man, Ole Budsberg of Iola, Wisconsin, came across Belle's advertisement in a Norwegian paper and found it intriguing. A widower, he was seeking companionship and a quiet life. He and Belle corresponded and found a mutual affection and life goals. Ole traveled to La Porte to court Belle in person and see the farm. He couldn't resist Belle's blue eyes, large bust, good Norwegian cooking, and the picturesque and prosperous estate. A week later, he returned to Iola to sell his assets. In good spirits, he said goodbye to his sons and promised to write once he was settled in his new home with his new wife.

When Ole arrived in La Porte, Belle met him at the station. They went to the bank together to cash in on a mortgage note on some land he owned, and they went back to the bank the following day to pick up the cash. That was the last time he was seen alive.

Ole's sons became concerned when they didn't hear from their father, so they sent a letter to Belle to inquire after their father's whereabouts. The letter was returned as undeliverable.

When the mortgage note came due and remained unpaid, the bank in Iola sent an inquiry to the bank in La Porte. The bank's cashier, not having seen Ole for some time, drove out to the Gunness farm to find him. An inhospitable Belle answered the door but refused him entry. Rather curtly, she said she had taken Ole to the train station, where he caught a train for Oregon, and she hadn't spoken to him since. She closed the door, ending the matter.

The banker relayed what happened to Ole's sons, who knew something had to be terribly wrong. They tried one more time, contacting the sheriff. But he assured them that nothing was amiss at the widow's house. They didn't feel assured.

5

Boundless Opportunities for an Enterprising Woman

BELLE, EVER THE ENTREPRENEUR, WAS SUSPECTED OF OPER-
ating several side businesses in addition to running the farm and
corresponding with would-be suitors. She first considered resur-
recting the lucrative baby farm operation she'd run in Chicago, but
in the rural areas surrounding La Porte, children weren't an extra
burden; they could eat what was grown on the farm and even at
very young ages could be a help with chores and childcare.

As mentioned previously, connections were made between Belle
and several matrimonial agencies. This isn't surprising, as Belle
likely employed a broker to help her with finding appropriate suitors in addition to advertising in newspapers. However, the agencies she chose to do business with were later found to be running
scams—which really shouldn't have been a surprise either. Male
customers were sent a photo of a pretty woman and a variation of
the following letter: "Handsome young lady worth $25,000 wants
acquaintance of honorable gentleman; early marriage; no objection
to poor man if honest. Address Mrs. W, 697 Fulton Street, Chicago."
Of course, that lady would no longer be available, but those paying
a $5 registry fee were provided with a choice of other women. With
her head for the business of love, it makes sense that she would
align herself with such a lucrative business.

Belle Gunness with her daughters, Lucy and Myrtle, and baby Philip in a photo taken three years before the fire. *Photo courtesy of the La Porte County Historical Society.*

St. Joseph, Michigan, a lovely lakeside town located where the St. Joseph River flows into Lake Michigan some thirty-nine miles from La Porte and connected not just by roads but also by interurbans, housed one such matrimonial agency. Run by J. S. Blackney, this affinity agency as it was called scouted prospects for Belle. Blackney described a wealthy widow in possession of a large farm who was eligible for matrimony and sent would-be suitors to La Porte. What isn't clear is what Belle's end of the deal was. Though there was some speculation.

In the early years of the twentieth century, abortions were illegal but available. Doctors even advertised, though somewhat subtly. There was no talk of ending a pregnancy but instead promises of restoring menses. A pregnant woman could also try to end her pregnancy by taking pills made from a combination of ingredients such as tansy oil, pennyroyal, rue, ergot, and even sometimes opium. The pills sometimes worked, sometimes damaged internal organs, and sometimes resulted in seizures and death.

It was a triple bind for a woman—she couldn't use birth control because very little existed at that time and it was illegal anyway, she was reviled if she had an out-of-wedlock child, and even if she wanted to keep the baby, she likely couldn't afford to rear a child on her own. What adoption and social services existed were overwhelmed with abandoned children—a serious and tragic problem. In the mid-1800s in New York City alone, there were thirty thousand homeless children who took to the streets, stealing food, shoplifting goods to pay for a meal, begging money from those passing by, joining gangs, and often ending up in jail. Female children often found themselves lured into prostitution, even at a very young age—some men were willing to pay a high price for young, innocent children. Young virgins were worth their weight in gold, and many a young girl lost her virginity several times over. Within a short time, they ended up diseased, aged beyond their years, often addicted to drink or drugs, and emotionally wrecked.

To add to a woman's problems, if her attempts to terminate her pregnancy made her ill, doctors would likely refuse treatment unless she confessed to having tried to abort her child. It didn't help that the Comstock chastity laws in 1873 prevented the dissemination of information about birth control and wouldn't be amended even slightly until 1916 when Margaret Sanger was arrested for opening a birth control clinic. Before that, married couples could be arrested in their own bedrooms for practicing family planning.

Of course, it really didn't stop people from having sex—extraordinarily little does—and then trying to terminate pregnancies. It was estimated that one in five pregnancies were aborted in the 1800s.

As with alcohol during Prohibition, where there's a market, there are enterprising people willing to meet the demand. It was rumored that Belle filled this necessary niche. She was ideally situated for this discreet operation, living in a large, isolated home within convenient proximity to Chicago. Neighbors noted men in large cars with young women arriving at all hours of the day and night.

Belle was not a physician, but that was often the case. Women were desperate. A pregnant unmarried woman was banished from society, often even her parents' home. A woman who traded her looks and youth for favors, both monetary and otherwise, would be out of work if she were pregnant, and prostitution was not a career that lent itself to motherhood.

Men, too, favored abortions, though they legislated against them. Indiana in the 1800s had several notorious abortion cases. One involved a dental student who murdered pretty Pearl Bryant from Greencastle after she told him she was pregnant and wanted him to marry her. Instead, he cut off her head (which was never found) and left her body in a field across the Ohio River in Kentucky. She was identified by her new shoes, which had been bought at a store hundreds of miles away. He and his accomplice went to the gallows, but even while waiting for the trapdoor to open, he refused to provide some degree of closure to her family by revealing what he had done with her head. Now people visiting her grave in Greencastle leave pennies, the head side up, on her grave as a show of respect.

A rich and respected businessman in Marshall, Indiana—not far from La Porte—hired a doctor who specialized in the restoration of menses to take care of his mistress's unborn child. Unfortunately, septic shock set in and she died a long and painful death. Both doctor and businessman were arrested but then freed, and the case, once garnering intense interest in newspapers throughout the region, suddenly was no longer reported on. Such is the way with money and, some would say, women who were no longer wanted.

Many abortions took place in unsanitary conditions by those who had no medical experience, and deadly outcomes were frequent. Penicillin wasn't developed until 1928, and abortion deaths due to septic shock, severe infection, and massive blood loss were common. However, that was no concern of Belle's; she was paid for her services whether the patient lived or died. If she lost a patient here and there, well, there was plenty of ground to cover up the mistake—for a fee, of course.

With her many acres, Belle was in a position to take on another business venture. It could be supposed that she had moved to La Porte at the request of Levee gangs to operate a body farm and to help gals in trouble. This could have simply been a continuation of the services she provided in Chicago—after all, no one knew what really happened to all those children who disappeared from her care. Neighbors, and later the police, came to believe that the basement and grounds of her house in Austin might be a cemetery.

Chicago was a hotbed of murder and mayhem, and gangs polished off business rivals, stoolies, unwanted girlfriends, those who knew too much, and just about anyone else they took a disliking to. Call it wholesale homicide. If mobsters weren't enough, there were also two serial killers operating in Chicago at the same time Belle was adopting and disposing of young children.

Herman Mudgett, best known as H. H. Holmes, used Chicago as his home base. Holmes was a University of Michigan medical student who jettisoned healing and instead turned to torture and murder. While Holmes confessed to only twenty-seven murders, some tallies have reached as high as two hundred, most of whom were never found.

One might think it would be difficult to hide a large number of bodies in a city. But Holmes was wickedly clever and hired Benjamin Pitzel (sometimes spelled Pitezel) to build a unique building designed specifically for his murderous purposes. Crisscrossed with secret and soundproof rooms, trapdoors, hidden passages, and doors that locked from the outside, it had everything an efficient murderer could ask for, including gas jets to asphyxiate victims and a kiln for cremating their bodies. After Pitzel finished this masterpiece, Holmes murdered him and then went on to murder several of his children in case they knew too much.

Holmes didn't just murder for expediency, he liked knowing his victims were suffering locked up in his small, cramped death chambers. As they were dying, Holmes was often enjoying a gourmet meal at a fine restaurant, probably made more delectable as he thought about their suffering. One such victim was a young and pretty woman who had been his lover. In the murder castle's crypt he had put her in, the police found evidence of her bare feet pounding against the casket's lid, and her tiny fists were bruised from trying to make it through the concrete as she slowly suffocated to death.

A great admirer of Holmes, and possibly his helper, Johann Hoch was a German immigrant with an amazing ability to convince women to surrender their life savings and often, albeit more unwillingly, their lives. The lucky ones were those he just abandoned, often penniless. Like Belle, Hoch used matrimonial agencies and advertisements in native language newspapers to lure lonely women desperate for love and attention who had money enough to arouse his interest.

Also like Belle, the plump, middle-aged, plain-faced Hoch wasn't particularly attractive. But he was charming and knew how to present himself as a prosperous suitor. He also was a devout student of mesmerism and hypnosis, having taken a mail-order class on the subject from a master mesmerist in Jackson, Michigan. Wherever Hoch went—and he moved around a lot—he carried his books on hypnotism and mesmerism along with his diploma showing that he had become a master hypnotist. Was it a coincidence that a book on hypnosis was found later when Belle's farmhouse was destroyed by fire?

Hoch, like Holmes, was said to have dispatched thirty or more women. He was such a Holmes wannabe that he spent time in Cincinnati, most likely in the house where Holmes had lived, and there killed several women. He also owned a home near the murder castle. In both locations he managed to murder several women—another way of keeping up.

Holmes was the first to get caught, walking up the steps to the gallows on May 7, 1896, just nine days before he turned thirty-five. Of the twenty-seven people he confessed to murdering, nine were confirmed. If Hoch had used Holmes's place to dispose of his victims, then he was out of luck after that. The pressure might have been on to find a new body disposal system.

Hoch knew enough of medicine—and forensic science was so limited back then—that his victims were diagnosed as expiring from stomach ailments (maybe in the way of some of Belle's children, including Caroline and Axel). Families and the local law might have been suspicious, but Hoch was often back on the road, using a different name, before his victim's body was in the ground. But how many wives or girlfriends can a man lose to stomach ailments before people got suspicious? And Hoch faced a dilemma: where to stow the bodies.

Though we'll probably never know for sure, future reports would indicate that Belle and Hoch may have interacted. They both used matrimonial agencies, they lived in Chicago around the same time (though, granted, Chicago is a big place), and they both operated their murderous schemes in Northwest Indiana as well. They both used their nationalities to lure romantic victims from similar backgrounds and neither minded getting their hands bloody. But while Hoch didn't have a body disposal setup, Belle did.

Hoch's murderous sojourn through Northern Indiana convinced many that he and Belle were partners in crime: Hoch seduced women into marriage, took their cash, ended their lives, and shipped them to Belle's farm. Belle, in turn, dismembered the bodies, buried them with quicklime, and collected a fee for her trouble.

Certainly, the goings-on under the moonlight at the Gunness farm were enough to raise such suspicions. Carriages often arrived in the middle of the night, and large trunks and boxes were dropped off at the house. And, of course there were late-night visitors who entered her home never to be seen again.

Clyde Sturgis and Leo Wade were deliverymen accustomed to the Gunness home. They hauled trunks and boxes marked variously with "potatoes" and "wallpaper" to Belle's front door, often after dark. Sometimes they were not allowed past the threshold. Other times, they were ordered to bring the trunks inside but with the lights off so they couldn't see and had to be led by Belle through the dark rooms. Clyde recalled later that the trunks were old, heavy, and strongly corded. But when he tried to help out by uncording the trunks, Belle berated him, saying he should mind his own business and pushed him out the door.

The Laphams, just by way of being neighbors, couldn't help but notice the deliveries made to the Gunness farm. One day a man drove his wagon up to the farm and unloaded a box from its back. Large enough to contain a casket, it emitted a foul odor.

The box contained a dead dog, Belle told Frank Lapham, and the man had offered to pay her five dollars to bury it on her land. Belle gave him permission to bury the beast in her orchard. Five dollars at that time comes to about $155 in today's money, a large sum back then when many people earned just a dollar a day.

When the man left, he took the box with him. Belle told Frank that she questioned the man about this and he explained he didn't want to dig a hole big enough for the whole box, so he just buried the remains instead.

Frank thought this all was a bit unusual, but he thought it even odder when Belle added that she was telling him this just in case he happened to hear rumors about strange things going about on her farm.

Of course, by then, La Porte was full of curiosity about Belle and what was happening on the Gunness farm. Even the mayor, Lemuel Darrow, had a story. Belle reported that she thought a woman and a man had killed an infant and buried it. "She showed the policeman the hole, but it didn't contain anything," Darrow said. "All around she impressed me as being insane or being actuated by some hidden motive that I could not understand."

Belle's stories seemed designed to throw others off the scent—to prevent them from understanding what they were seeing: a murderess in their quiet small town.

6

Jennie Olsen

JENNIE OLSEN WAS A SWEET-NATURED BEAUTY WITH THICK flaxen hair, a shy smile, and a healthy, sun-kissed complexion. At sixteen, she was turning heads in La Porte, and she had several suitors, including Emil Greening. Hired by Belle as a farmhand, Emil lived and worked on the property. He and Jennie lived as brother and sister, sharing meals, often doing chores together, and finding time to talk about all things. At night, after dinner, Jennie and her siblings would retire to their bedrooms in the main part of the house and Emil would climb the stairs to his room in the wooden addition above the kitchen.

Jennie had few friends except for Lucy and Myrtle because her mother intimidated others so much they stayed away, but those who met her liked her. She was a dreamy girl who spent what little spare time she had reading, but she was unaccustomed to speaking her thoughts and feelings. Belle's controlling behavior probably helped drive the independence out of her. Emil's gentleness and caring led Jennie away from her recessive solitude. He became her confidant. She had never had one before. Myrtle and Lucy were too much younger, and her other friends like Harriet and Cora hadn't been allowed to spend much time with her. She would have liked to confide in May, her sister, but now she hardly ever saw her father and siblings. And so the bond between Emil and Jennie, evident to all, continued to grow. Whether it was romantic on Jennie's part

Jennie Olsen. *Photo courtesy of the La Porte County Historical Society.*

is hard to know because there was another suitor who came courting as well—John Weidner, a strong young man who worked in a local carriage factory.

Jennie told Emil about her real family and how she sometimes yearned to visit them. But she felt Belle's disapproval when she talked about them, and Belle was not a woman to cross.

There had been a time, when she was very little, Belle often took Jennie to visit her father and siblings. Before each visit, Belle dressed Jennie in the nicest clothes and brushed her hair until it shone, putting a pretty ribbon in it. But those visits had grown fewer, and when Jennie's father, who had remarried, demanded that Belle return his daughter (there had never been a formal adoption), she refused, and relations turned stormy.

After Belle moved to La Porte, Jennie visited her family back in Chicago and seemed to be having a great time—until Belle came to visit. After she left, Jennie asked to cut the visit short, saying she wanted to be back on the farm. The Olsens believed Belle had bullied Jennie into going home sooner because she was jealous and afraid that Jennie would remain with them permanently, said May.

After that visit, Jennie only saw her Olsen relatives once, when May came to the farm for a visit. As May recalled it later, she'd barely entered the farmhouse, let alone taken off her hat and listened to Jennie play a tune on the piano, before Belle was ushering her out the door. It was obvious she was not welcome.

By talking to Emil, examining her feelings and her observations, Jennie came to realize she'd been manipulated by Belle into rejecting her biological family. Had she made a mistake in trying to please Belle by severing those ties? But when Belle became angry, Jennie became overcome with dread and fear. Her only thought then was to placate and please Belle and make her nice again.

Those weren't the only losses Jennie discussed with Emil. There was Mads, who had been a father to her. She told Emil of the games Mads played with the three of them; they all adored him and his ever-cheerful demeanor. She understood that Belle's seriousness most likely came from caring for her and her three siblings as well as tending the farm on her own, but she wished Belle could sometimes be lighthearted like Mads had been.

And there were Harriet Danielson and Cora Larson, her two best friends in Chicago. Even though it had been years since they'd moved from Chicago, Jennie and Harriet continued to exchange letters. At one point, she wrote Harriet asking if she'd come visit the farm in La Porte, telling her how beautiful it was, about her adorable little brother whom Harriet had never met, and how they would have the best time. It was so easy to get here, she said; trains ran from Chicago to La Porte all the time.

Belle, Jennie said, wanted Harriet to come as well. Reading the letter back in Chicago, Harriet wondered at this, thinking it odd that Belle would want to see her as she'd always made it plain that she disliked Harriet and tried to keep Jennie away from her. But even beyond that, Harriet felt uneasy in a way she couldn't articulate about the invitation.

During the time she'd known Jennie in Chicago, she'd seen children come and go in the Sorenson house, including the first helpless and sweet little Lucy. She had heard her parents and neighbors talk about their suspicions about those children and about the deaths of Caroline and Axel, who both died before their first birthdays. She also had been there the day that Mads died. He was so alive when they first came to the house, and then, suddenly, by the time they arrived back at Jennie's with their bags of apples, he was dead, and Belle was carrying on. She had never thought Belle liked Mads that well—she ordered him around and treated him with disdain, complaining he didn't make enough money. Harriet, like many people in the neighborhood, found it difficult to believe that she was really that upset.

Unnerved and wondering if Belle wanted to harm her, Harriet wrote back saying she couldn't make it. She would write several more times, but she never heard again from Jennie. She couldn't understand why, as Jennie wasn't the sort to hold a grudge; surely she wasn't ignoring her because she could not make the trip. Always suspicious of Belle, Harriet wondered if she was keeping her letters from Jennie.

It was no secret that Belle was often mean to Jennie. Sure, all the children were well fed, had nice clothes to wear to church and school, and had that wonderful pony cart, but at home, in private, they saw Belle's dark side.

Mailman D. J. Hunter recalled seeing Jennie Olsen frequently. She drove the cows home late in the afternoon as he delivered the mail to residents on his route encompassing McClung Road. She walked barefoot on the dusty road, wearing a faded, torn dress that came only halfway to her ankles despite the fact that she was now a young woman and should be wearing long skirts.

Fish Trap Lake. *Photo courtesy of the Steve Shook Collection.*

"She was shy and serious," he said. "I felt sorry for her, and I always made it a point to speak to her."

Jennie would return the greeting, and according to D. J., her big blue eyes brightened at his friendliness, seemingly pleased to have anyone take notice of her.

"At other times, I would see her working out in the garden. She had to work hard, poor girl, but once or twice just before time to drive home the cows, I would see her sitting, reading by the fence along the road, and I often wondered what it was that she was reading."

Jess Dickinson, a well-known wrestler, was fishing at Fishtrap Lake when he saw Jennie, leading a cow, enter the woods by the edge of the lake across the road from her home. As he watched, Jennie sat down by a tree and started reading a book, often glancing up to keep an eye on the cow. Dickinson wasn't the only one to see the girl. Looking up from his fishing pole, he watched as Belle snuck up on Jennie and then began beating her on the calves of her legs.

After Belle left, Dickinson walked over to check on Jennie.

The beatings happen often, Jennie told him. Pulling aside her clothing, she showed him marks from previous beatings.

The beatings weren't enough to keep Jennie from spending time with John Weidner though. Belle was used to controlling Jennie, and she was angry that Jennie and John were growing closer. It wouldn't do for him to propose, and Belle expected him to do so soon. Women married young back then, particularly in rural communities, and Jennie was sixteen. She might even get pregnant and then have to wed. It had to be stopped.

Belle had been cordial toward John at first, but now she turned against him. She told Jennie she couldn't see him anymore. For once, Jennie let her anger show.

"She had better let me go with you," she told John, "or I'll tell something."

As Jennie grew more assertive, Belle began watching her interactions with Emil more carefully as well. Jennie had told Emil about the eighteen hundred dollars that was to be given to her on her eighteenth birthday and that Belle was holding it for her.

Emil, for his part, seemed to now view Belle with suspicion and wariness, and though his behavior was as pleasant as ever, Belle was a keen observer and could tell. What else had Jennie told him? What had he seen? He might have been a farmhand, but he was smart.

Belle did her best to protect her children from the details of her business endeavors, but she could no longer count on Jennie to keep her observations to herself.

Belle suddenly announced that she had decided to send Jennie to college, surprising everyone. She began at once to make beautiful clothing. Jennie would need a new wardrobe, of course, as she certainly didn't want to look the part of a dirty farm girl when she went to Los Angeles, California.

Belle watched Jennie silently, unaware of the grim look she wore as she saw the quick succession of emotions pass on her adopted daughter's face. With a little shake, Belle cleared her mind and returned to her sewing.

Jennie tried not to show it, but she didn't want to go all the way to Los Angeles. She'd be leaving so much behind and going to a big city where she didn't know anyone. She would be so far away from Emil and John and her darling siblings. She was practically a mother to them as Belle was often so busy the child-rearing was left to Jennie. How would they fare without her? Who would protect them from Belle's anger?

Word of Jennie's college adventure spread quickly, and several people visited to wish Jennie well. Belle showed all of them the beautiful clothes she'd made for Jennie as well as a cloak she said she'd bought in Chicago for $50—an extravagant amount for anyone but particularly a farmer's daughter.

Belle avoided giving a departure date but said that she had arranged for a professor to collect Jennie and escort her along the long journey to the college—curiously not by train but by horse and buggy. A journey like that, across the Great Plains and the mountains in the winter in a buggy didn't make sense. Even with two strong horses, they couldn't make more than twenty or twenty-five miles a day, and they'd constantly have to find a place to stay and switch out horses. If it snowed—and it would, it was winter after all—they'd be at risk of getting stuck and freezing to death. And besides, California was some two thousand miles away. Even at twenty-five miles a day, it would take almost two-thirds of a year to get there. No, it didn't make any sense at all. Why not just take a train? It would take only a few days. Odd, people thought, very odd indeed.

When John stopped by to visit Jennie ten days before Christmas, she must have given in to Belle's plans because she told him she was leaving for Los Angeles, where she'd be going to school. She asked John to visit her the following Sunday to say goodbye. He promised he would.

There were other visitors to the farmhouse. Belle's friend, the young Julius G. Truelson, who lived in New York City but had previously resided in Chicago, was there for a while. Julius was said to be the son of a wealthy piano manufacturer, and the family lived in a very nice apartment in New York City. The two had met several years earlier, and he often helped out with chores on the farm when he was around. Belle had convinced him that she was studying to be a midwife and sometimes needed help with medical mistakes. Truelson didn't stay long. He had just gotten in trouble in Fort Wayne, Indiana, under an assumed name and his family once again had to buy his way out of trouble.

On a snowy Christmas Eve, the professor and two other people, a woman and a man, arrived at the house, and Emil was sent to sleep in the barn. When Emil awoke and walked over to the house,

GUNNESS PONY.

One of Belle's ponies. *Photo courtesy of the La Porte County Historical Society.*

Belle told him Jennie had already left with the professor and his wife earlier that morning. She was on her way to Los Angeles.

Why, Emil wondered, didn't Jennie come to the barn to say goodbye to him?

A heavy snow was falling on the Sunday that Jennie had asked John to stop by. So he hired a cutter and made his way to the farm. Belle came to the door and could barely hide her glee in telling him Jennie was already gone. He asked Belle for her address, which she gave him.

Like Emil, John couldn't understand why Jennie hadn't said goodbye or somehow gotten word to him that she was leaving early.

John wrote several letters to Jennie, but never heard back. Nine months later, seeing Belle in town, he mentioned not having gotten even one letter from her. Belle laughed and told him that she'd heard he had married and had written to tell Jennie just that.

It was my brother who got married, John said, and he asked Belle to have Jennie write him. Of course, she promised. He never heard from Jennie.

Emil also wrote several letters to Jennie, but his letters went unanswered as well.

Belle occasionally produced a letter she said Jennie had written to her, and as she read it aloud for others to hear, she would start to sniffle as if she were going to cry with sorrow. Of course, she never let anyone see the letter.

But no one else—not her two suitors, siblings, or friends in Chicago—ever received a reply to the countless letters they sent. It was like she didn't exist anymore. Over the next few months, even the location of where Jennie was going to school changed. Some still heard she was in Los Angeles, while Belle told others she was attending a college in Minnesota. But that was Belle. She never told one story when two or more would do.

7

The Rivals

WITH JENNIE GONE AND NO WORD FROM HER, EMIL FELT HE had been abandoned and found the Gunness farm to be lonely and depressing. And Belle was acting strangely. One night, during a thunderstorm, Emil awoke to the sound of his doorknob being twisted back and forth as if someone was trying to get in. He'd locked it when he went to bed that night. Determined to see who was trying to gain entrance to his room, he quietly walked to the door, turned the lock quickly, and pulled it open. In the hallway, Belle, dressed in a nightgown, was backing away.

What's going on, Emil asked.

Belle replied that the storm had unsettled her, and she had gotten confused. This, of course, didn't make much sense to Emil. The bedrooms where Belle and her children stayed were in a different part of the house. Regaining her composure, Belle moved closer to Emil as if to enter his room. He sensed what she had in mind but had no interest in inviting her in, so he said he was tired and shut the door, making sure to lock it once again.

He would later tell his mother what had happened. It was shocking and shameful, she thought, that this fifty-year-old woman would want to crawl in bed with her young son.

It was, Emil decided, time to move on. Why not try homesteading out west, he thought. Jennie could write to him there just as

A postcard showing a man petting the horse belonging to the Gunness children. *Photo courtesy of the Steve Shook Collection.*

easily, if she ever did write. And actually, he'd be a lot closer to her if she wanted him to come visit. So he gave notice, packed up, and left.

This was just as well as far as Belle was concerned. She was angry at him for rejecting her and tired of his constant moping and questions about Jennie. She would need a new hired hand, of course, but she already had her eye on someone.

Thirty-seven-year-old Ray Lamphere was a drunk and a dullard who worked odd jobs about town. He was born into a prestigious family, the son of a justice of the peace. However, his father lost the family's money and respect at the bottom of a bottle, and Ray seemed determined to follow in his father's footsteps. He spent most of his time in saloons, gambling and drinking away any money he earned.

Belle approached him in town one day and in her direct manner stated simply that she had been watching him and wanted him to come work for her. Soon, Ray had moved into Emil's old room above the kitchen and was a regular sight on the Gunness farm.

Ray was much more than just a farmhand though. As he boasted to his drinking companions, Belle entered his room that first night with her dark hair loose, contrasting against her flowing white nightgown, and in the darkened shadows, the years disappeared

Ray Lamphere. *Photo courtesy of the La Porte County Historical Society.*

from her face. She slipped into bed beside him, and, unlike Emil, Ray didn't object. She found not only a convenient lover but also a besotted man who would do whatever she asked of him.

Night after night, before sneaking away to her own room at daybreak, Belle made Ray feel special, like he was the only man she could ever love. She was soft and gentle and purred beneath his attentions. When she had to distance herself to attend to her business affairs, she gave him little presents to make up for it. Once, she even gave him a silver watch.

The whispered promises and shiny trinkets kept Ray in his place for a while, but as Belle's spell deepened, so too did Ray's jealousy. When Belle's suitors came to the farm, they required all her attention. She had little patience for Ray's complaints and often made him relinquish his room to the visitors, both ensuring Ray did not upset her plans and reestablishing her position of power on the farm.

When banished to the barn, Ray's thoughts turned dark—not toward Belle but toward the men who expected to share Belle's property, wealth, and bed. She told him it was business, and he knew she was taking their cash and their possessions, including the fine watch she had given him. When it came time to dispose of these sycophants, Ray felt no remorse. They did not love Belle as he did. They were merely parasites in search of a host.

Ray proved himself to Belle over and over again, but it seemed to never be enough. She continued writing letters to other men. In the bars, he heard talk from those who had seen her in the post office, standing there writing responses to the letters she had just received. This was a woman who didn't waste a moment in ensnaring new men, and Ray didn't like it at all.

Sometimes when he was exiled to the barn, Ray instead made his way to a ramshackle house by the railroad depot where Liz Smith lived. She always welcomed Ray into her bed. Belle was more than a decade older than Ray, but that was nothing compared to the age difference between Liz and Ray. She was in her mid-seventies, and time had worn her down. String-bean thin, she dressed in layers and layers of old clothing, making her look almost like a scarecrow. It was enough to scare the children who passed by her home when she was sitting on her porch—until they discovered that though odd looking, she was kind.

But this was Liz Smith in the early 1900s. In her younger days, she had been considered the most beautiful woman in Northern Indiana—some even said all of Indiana. Outspoken and feisty, Liz would have been a heroine in today's movies and novels. She was a woman who did what she wanted no matter the scandal, and her behavior invited every sort of notice. Newspaper accounts recorded her feuds, court dates, and how she even once took a hatchet to newspaper editor Arthur B. Reed because she didn't like what he'd written about her. He avoided the sharp edge, though his newsroom took some hits, and was pretty nonchalant about the whole incident that had him running around the pressroom to avoid her. After all, he'd faced her anger before.

Chasing Arthur around with a hatchet was nothing for Liz. Married to a former Civil War soldier and the mother of two daughters, she was involved in a tempestuous affair with Leonidas Cole, a successful attorney, the son of one of La Porte's earliest founding families, a member of the Presbyterian church where he took an active interest in Sunday school, and a mason. During the Civil War, he enlisted as a private and quickly rose to the rank of captain, participating in the battles of Shiloh, Stone River, Chickamauga, Lookout Mountain, and Mission Ridge.

A beauty and a hero. What a pair.

Many were outraged by the immorality of the two. And not just because Leonidas, whose stately house is one of many mansions still lining La Porte's Indiana Avenue, was married with children but because Liz was the daughter of slaves. Leonidas was said to be the father of one of her two daughters. The truth of that lies in the fact that he gave her a large sum of money for the girl's education and care.

Liz was not without other admirers as well. In her early years, many white men pursued her, but none would have dared marry her. After all, Indiana outlawed cohabitation and marriage between different races, including not only African Americans but also Native Americans, Filipinos, Asians, East Indians, and native Hawaiians until the law was overturned in 1965.

Leonidas got religion, organized a temperance league, and was converted at a revival, confessing his sin of fornication with Liz in front of a huge crowd. She didn't like this one bit and was so angered that she horsewhipped him on La Porte's public square until he promised to make it up to her.

Or maybe she hung him upside down from a second-floor window, depending on which story you believe. But do know this, Smith was capable of both. Besides her public spats with Leonidas, she was known to throw things, and if that didn't work, she would fire a gun over people's heads to make her point. She had a temperament similar to that of Belle, and the two were said to be friends—their tendency toward making their viewpoints vociferously known and their willingness to take Ray into their beds creating a bond of sorts.

Besides being horsewhipped, Leonidas paid dearly for his relationship with Liz in other ways. Newspapers throughout the Midwest reported that Judge Gresham revoked Leonidas Cole's appointment as a United States commissioner "on account of Cole's fondness for a colored woman."

While Leonidas may have embraced sobriety and religion, Liz still seemed to have a lot of emotion invested in their affair and wasn't above demanding her ex-lover's attention in any way she could. Though local newspapers tiptoed politely around the affair, Chicago reporters were not so kind. She was arrested for walking alongside him on the street, and then in another incident, she again was in court for sending him obscene postcards.

All this was probably more than enough for Lucetta Van Meter Hinkle Cole, married for thirty-four years to Leonidas and the mother of his three children, Alta May, Persa Lin (nicknamed Percy), and Lina. As for Leonidas, he cracked. Showing symptoms of insanity, he was diagnosed as suffering from acute mania and sent for treatment at the Northern Indiana Hospital for the Insane in Logansport. The newly opened sanitarium was also known as Longcliff, a reference to its tranquil location on a high bluff overlooking the scenic Wabash River where it was located.

Leonidas was not expected to recover, and he didn't, dying on Monday, February 23, 1891. By then, his family appeared to have moved from La Porte. Only his son, Percy, returned home for the funeral.

Besides the loss of Leonidas, who was probably the love of her life given the passion she showed at his rejection of her and her

The Northern Indiana Hospital for the Insane was known as Longcliff because of its beautiful location on the banks of the Wabash River in Logansport, Indiana. *Photo courtesy of Wikimedia Commons.*

inability to let go, Liz had also lost her mother, who was nicknamed Mother Armstead and was well regarded in La Porte; she died at age 104. Liz's husband and father were also gone. Both of her daughters had predeceased her, one dying in high school and the other marrying and moving to Chicago, where she too died. Neither left grandchildren for Liz to cherish.

Liz was now alone, and the beauty that had made a man lose his mind was gone. But her ferocious temperament remained. And though she lived in squalor, she was a well-to-do woman, the owner of seven properties—though none were kept up—and she had a lot of money in the bank. She'd been passionate and given to histrionics, yet she'd also been wise and saved much of the money given to her by those long-ago admirers.

As for Ray, he was spending more and more time in the saloons, drinking too much and telling everyone who would listen that he was going to marry Belle, that he had in fact already married her. Most took this for what it was—the lovesick ramblings of a drunkard. Others found it to be fodder for town gossip. He also came to believe that he deserved some of the cash Belle was raking in from her suitors and started demanding that she share some of the loot. Given all that he did for her, it was a fair demand.

There was another rival for Belle's attention—and maybe affection. One she might have, if rumors were true, depended on as much as she did Ray: the driver of the red roadster often seen parked outside her home, Sheriff Smutzer.

Belle was unhappy with Ray's behavior. He was becoming more trouble than he was worth. But still, she had to tread lightly. Though Ray's obsession combined with his drinking made for precarious footing, he was still useful. She just had to manipulate the situation appropriately while continuing to lure men and their liquidated assets to her doorstep.

Some men were eager to wed the wealthy widow landowner and cared little about building a relationship through letters. They felt the direct approach was better and traveled to La Porte as quickly as they could. Others required a bit more convincing.

Andrew Helgelien was one such suitor. Belle had been writing at least a letter every week to the forty-nine-year-old wheat farmer from Aberdeen, South Dakota, for well over a year. Andrew had satisfactorily answered when Belle questioned the amount of money he planned to invest in their future together, but he also brought to the table something Belle hadn't experienced in quite some time: a challenge.

At first, Belle's letters to Andrew tried to tempt him with the magnificence of the estate, "74 acres of land" that were "right in the midst of where the rich people have their fine summer houses." Belle, of course, was exaggerating a bit as she only owned forty-three acres. She went on to say, "All kinds of fruit trees abound here and good new houses with all improvements and fine boulevard roads." Indiana was a dream, "mild in the winter and not so very warm in the summer, with plenty of rain and no storms and the land is all good so we can raise anything." Being so close to Chicago, the land in La Porte was "going up all the time. There are very many who are almost millionaires now by having bought pieces of land a few years ago and have doubled the prices many times and sold out the land in small lots to businesspeople in Chicago for summer homes."

She caught Andrew's interest, but not enough to persuade him to "come as soon as possible," as she advised. She tried appealing to his

Andrew Helgelien. *Photo courtesy of the La Porte County Historical Society.*

vanity: "Many thousand thanks for both your letter and photograph card. I have read the letter many times and studied the picture much also. I have now so much confidence and interest in our correspondence, especially when I know that you are such an understanding and good Norwegian man." When Andrew continued to drag his feet, Belle knew he was going to be different from the rest.

Andrew was different. The broad-shouldered, thick-necked Norwegian had spent ten years in prison for robbing a village post and then burning down the building. He was cautious in his dealings with Belle. And he was very close to his brother Asle and his sister Anna. Most important, Andrew would lead Belle to her downfall.

But in the months leading up to their meeting, Belle saw only the prize. She played on his nostalgia for Norway by promising to make him meals of Norwegian codfish, cream pudding, and waffles, and painting herself as a "genuine Norwegian with brown Norwegian hair and blue eyes . . . who does not bother herself much about all these fine Americans."

Still she could not hook Andrew. On the contrary, it seemed that Andrew had hooked Belle. He made promises to come but then postponed his departure several times, costing Belle more emotion than she was used to investing. Her letters began to show her anxieties: "You do not know how downhearted I became when I read that you could not come for Christmas and that you have decided to remain up there all winter." And again the following year: "Now it is already the 25th of September and last year at this time I waited for you and yet you haven't come to me. . . . It seems as if you will never get your belongings in order up there." As always, Belle continued to encourage him to sell everything he owned and come at once to her side with the cash, telling no one of his move so they might have a little time alone together at first.

At last, Belle had had enough. She wrote to him with the directive to "make up your mind as soon as possible as to what you really intend to do." This worked. On Friday, January 3, 1908, Belle met Andrew at the depot in La Porte.

Andrew didn't intend to stay long; he had only come to scope out the situation in La Porte and meet Belle in person. He had asked neighbors to look after his livestock and told his brother Asle he'd be home in a week. He had taken Belle's advice and hadn't told anyone where he was going. However, he hadn't sold his farm or brought the money, sewn in the lining of his coat, as Belle had continuously asked him to do in her letters.

Belle gave Andrew Ray's bedroom and told Ray to sleep in the barn, and she and Andrew spent the weekend getting to know one another. Andrew liked what he saw regarding both the farm and

A drawing of several areas of Belle's home including the basement where she supposedly butchered her victims and then wrapped them in burlap bags filled with quicklime, termed by the press as the "Secret Bluebeard Chamber." *Photo courtesy of the La Porte Historical Society.*

Belle. Neighbors said the couple acted like lovers right away. Now that she had him, Belle was not planning to let him go.

On Monday, the pair went to the First National Bank in La Porte to make arrangements for money from Andrew's Aberdeen account to be sent to La Porte. When she found out it would take several days to receive the money, Belle argued for a faster transaction, but there was simply nothing the clerk could do. Belle set her jaw and left on Andrew's arm.

Ray was not at all happy about this new arrival. Though part of Belle's method of operation had typically been to sleep with the men who came to the farm, for some reason Ray was particularly jealous about Andrew's relationship with Belle. Belle spent all her time with Andrew and didn't give Ray even a sideways glance, much less a dalliance in the dark. One night as Ray and his friend John Rye rode past the farm and saw Andrew and Belle walking around the yard, Ray muttered darkly that "something was going to come off at the farm."

The next day, Ray told John that he'd drilled a hole into the parlor floor to spy on Andrew and Belle and overheard them plotting to kill Ray with chloral (chloral hydrate is a sedative). Andrew told Belle he didn't know the effect of chloral and suggested she use it on Ray's dog. The next morning, Ray said, he found his dog dead. (Later his story changed, and the dog had run away but came home a week later. Still, Ray insisted the dog had been poisoned.) Ray was drinking even more and had become paranoid now that he had lost favor with Belle.

The money finally arrived in La Porte, and Belle accompanied Andrew to the bank to collect it. The cashier suggested Andrew open an account and deposit the money for safekeeping. Belle insisted he take the full amount in cash. She was no longer in good humor; she had worked this mark for the better part of two years, and now she was getting merely a portion of his wealth. She chided herself for having given so much attention to the chase, but that was part of the business, and any good businesswoman knew when to cut her losses.

8

The Beginning of the End

IT WAS AROUND MIDNIGHT WHEN EB HILL PULLED HIS HACK to a stop in front of Belle's large brick house on the dark and deserted country road.

Hill's passenger, a pretty, well-dressed young woman he'd picked up at the railroad station about a mile away in La Porte, descended from the hack and walked up toward the darkened front door, following the instructions she'd been given, but when she knocked, no one answered.

She knew the widow was waiting for her, because the message she'd received said to arrive at midnight on January 14, 1908. Addie Landis was not a woman to be deterred, and as Eb watched, she walked back down the front steps. But instead of returning to the hack, she followed the walkway leading to the back of the house, disappearing into the inky blackness.

Minutes later, Eb heard shrieks coming from inside the house and the loud cracking sound of bolts being shot open. After climbing down from the driver's seat, he stood frozen for a moment, uncertain of what to do, when the door was flung open. There, silhouetted in the light streaming from inside the house, Addie was struggling to break free from Belle's grip. Belle, said to be able to carry two pigs, one under each arm, was a strong farm woman. But Addie in her panic and fear delivered a fierce shove, pushing Belle away, and ran down the steps.

She hadn't gotten very far when she fainted. Eb hurried to her prone figure and scooped her up. The widow, standing in the doorway, stared at the two of them for a long moment, and though she and Eb knew each other and their eyes met, neither said a word. Then Belle went back inside, slamming the door behind her. There was the loud noise of bolts being shot back into place, and as Eb watched, every light in the house went out, one by one, until all the windows were black.

Once in the hack, Addie became hysterical, screaming, "Save me! Save me!" as Eb flicked the reins, heading back to the train depot. By the time they arrived, Addie was somewhat calmer, and she boarded the train back to Chicago. Only months later, in the fall, after spending time at Longcliff—the same place Leonidas Cole was sent after his breakdown—and being treated by doctors was the traumatized woman able to tell her story.

Earlier that day, after visiting the bank with Andrew, Belle sent Ray on an errand out of town. Her cousin was sending her a horse, and Ray was to meet him in Michigan City, about twelve miles away. Belle was emphatic in her instructions to wait for her cousin, even if that meant Ray had to stay the night in Michigan City. Ray didn't like leaving Belle with Andrew but left as his mistress commanded, though he was not quiet in his grumblings.

Ray convinced his friend John Rye to come along for the ride, and the two set out in a cutter. When they arrived at the meeting place, Belle's cousin was nowhere to be found. They waited for a bit, but Ray's impatience grew to anger, and the two decided to douse his fire at a saloon. After a few drinks, they caught a vaudeville show.

Ray and John went back to the livery barn where they were supposed to meet Belle's cousin. There was still no sign of him. Fed up and thinking he had been ordered on a fool's errand, Ray told John he was going to go back to La Porte. The two caught an interurban car, and Ray jumped off at the icehouse switch near Belle's farm, telling John, "I'm going over and see what the old woman is doing. I'll see you later at the saloon."

Ray was geared up for a fight, but when Belle answered the door, she simply invited him in. Julius Truelson, an old acquaintance, was seated in the parlor with Andrew. Expecting Ray to be gone for the night, Belle had hired Julius for the evening's work. After greetings were made, the four played cards for a bit. Though Ray resented the prosperous farmer from South Dakota for taking his place in Belle's bed, he noticed a subtle shift in power in the room's atmosphere. Andrew, oblivious, played his hand and drank his beer. Ray began to relax and inwardly gloat. He now understood that Andrew was a walking dead man.

Belle excused herself to refresh their drinks and expertly slipped poison into Andrew's beer. After a few gulps, Andrew began to feel quite odd and begged Belle to call a doctor. When she didn't, he began to struggle to get up, and the men attempted to subdue him. Belle hit him over the head, and he fell unconscious. Ray and Julius carried him to the door of the butchery room, but Belle insisted on doing the work herself and told the two men to wait outside.

All three were so caught up in the moment that they didn't notice Addie Landis's tentative knock at the door. Receiving no response, Addie walked around the house toward the light in the back. She could not contain her exclamation of horror when she saw Belle cutting off Andrew's head, while Ray stood by with an open sack ready to receive the gruesome by-product. The two men just stood there, surprised. But Belle was quick. She followed Addie as the younger woman rushed toward the back door and got in front of her, blocking her exit. Addie turned and ran through the house. The front door's bolts had been put in place, but they hadn't been turned to catch in their holders. Belle would later curse herself for being so foolish. Addie yanked them open just as Belle laid one of her huge hands on her. But Belle's hands were slippery with blood and she couldn't hold fast. Addie evaded Belle's grasping hands, swung the heavy door open, and ran out onto the porch. Belle caught her once more, and the two stumbled out the door into the darkness.

At the sight of Eb, Belle was momentarily distracted, just long enough for Addie to give her an adrenaline-fueled shove, breaking free. She ran down the steps toward Eb but was overcome and fainted. Belle didn't move. She quickly calculated whether she could grab Addie from Eb and kill them both. Probably not as she knew Eb often carried a gun for protection from troublesome passengers. A gunshot this late at night might wake neighbors. Already Addie's screams seemed to have echoed through the still night. So, as she watched Eb pick up the girl, she shot him a menacing look of warning. Then without a word, Belle stomped back into the house and slammed the door behind her.

There was nothing to be done about Addie, so Belle set back to work, hurriedly now as she didn't know if they would go to the police and if Smutzer could protect her this time. While she methodically butchered Andrew's body, she decided on a plan. She would deny the girl's story and say she had caught her in the house trying to steal. That's what the fight had been about.

Clear now in her plan, she finished the job and distributed packages of Andrew's parts to Julius and Ray to bury. Julius was eager to leave the scene, unsure of what Addie Landis might tell Eb or the authorities. Belle paid him well for his work and sent him on his way. She joined Ray in the yard to oversee the completion of the job.

Addie wasn't the only witness to the goings-on that night. Two men from Michigan City were walking toward an acquaintance's farmhouse on that bright moonlit night when they saw the figures of a man and a woman in the side yard of Belle's house. Moving closer, they saw that it was Belle and Ray, working in the fenced enclosure. One of the men raised his hand, ready to shout a greeting, but a feeling overcame him—an internal warning that it was best to be quiet. He exchanged a look with his companion, who nodded understanding. They both sensed danger and, stepping deeper into the shadows, fell silent, watching as Belle carried a heavy burden from the house and dropped it in a hole. She sprinkled something over it, and then Ray began shoveling in dirt to fill the hole. The two men figured they were burying a dead animal. Yet they remained uncomfortable, so they tried to move soundlessly as they continued along their way.

With Andrew gone, Belle assumed her relationship with Ray would resume as normal. But something had snapped in Ray. He was no longer the lovesick lackey, ready to receive Belle's orders. Instead, he began demanding more money for his tasks and silence. Belle paid him fifty bucks, but he thought he should get thousands. He was a drunk, but he wasn't dumb. He had figured out how much money Belle was bringing in.

Then came the final straw: Ray was returning to Belle's one day and saw Sheriff Albert Smutzer's fancy red roadster—an expensive machine, much pricier than a county sheriff should be able to afford—sitting in front of Belle's house. Albert was coming down the stairs and didn't stop to chat, just murmured hello while keeping his hat low over his face.

Inside, Belle was complaining about the sheriff and how she had given him a thousand dollars to keep quiet and insinuating she had helped pay for his car. Of course, Ray had heard the rumors that the sheriff and Belle were lovers, and now the thought of Albert getting to spend time in Belle's bed and raking in a fancy car and a thousand bucks—when Ray only got fifty—was just too much.

Upset, Ray resorted to his typical pursuit—drinking. As he spent more and more time in a state of inebriation, he became a wild card. On February 3, following a dispute over money, Belle fired Ray. Furious, he left the farm without taking any of his belongings. But the problem Ray posed was far from a resolution.

Ray consulted Wirt Worden, a successful attorney who often helped Ray out of scrapes even though the handyman had no money. Wirt, who was partners with Samuel Lemuel, the mayor of La Porte—and interestingly, a cousin of Clarence Darrow—told him he had the right to retrieve his belongings. When Ray tried to do so, Belle ran him off the farm and then retaliated by telling the sheriff that Ray was harassing her. But it wasn't until she actually caught Ray on her property again that she could charge him with a crime.

Sending the message that Ray would not be welcome back, Belle hired another farmhand, Joe Maxson. She had learned her lesson though. She stayed out of Joe's bed, and Joe stayed out of her business. Joe was perfectly content to work hard, put his money in the bank, and relax by playing a little fiddle music in the evenings.

Still Ray came around. Belle tried a different tack and filed an affidavit declaring Ray to be insane. Belle cited his harassment, intoxication, and "extraordinary propensities," among a list of behavioral traits—silent, quiet, melancholy, seclusive, dull, profane, filthy, intemperate, sleepless, and criminal—to defend her judgment. Surely, she thought, that will get him locked up as crazy.

Dr. B. O. Boutwell, Dr. C. E. Burleson, and Dr. L. E. Annis, the trio of doctors who judged Ray's mental health, saw him in a different light, saying he was patient, clean, quiet, and neat, though slightly nervous. His memory was deemed good for both recent and remote events; his speech was intelligent and coherent. In other words, they found that Ray, though a nervous sort, was sane.

Belle next offered Ray fifty dollars to go away. He countered, claiming she owed him a thousand dollars for his assistance. She should have just paid him and wrote it down as overhead costs. But for some reason, despite all he had done for her, she just couldn't bring herself to do so. A bad business decision on her part indeed.

It was back to court again. Belle and Myrtle swore under oath they saw Ray hanging out in the hog pen, and when they went to chase him away, he nonchalantly cut the wires of the fence, pulled out the fence post, and sauntered off. When Wirt got him off after presenting an alibi, Belle ominously warned that the court would have blood on their hands if anything happened to her and her family.

Left with no other recourse shy of disposing of him, Belle had Ray arrested again for trespassing. Ray did not plead guilty and instead retained the services of attorney Worden again, who immediately filed for a change of venue. Wirt was a short, stout, good-hearted, and good-looking man who would prove to be Ray's rock for some time to come. People wondered who was paying the attorney's fees. Some were sure it was Liz Smith.

At the trial, the line of questioning took a turn in a direction Belle had not seen coming. During cross-examination, Wirt went straight for the throat. He asked Belle about the death of her first husband and whether she profited much from the insurance money. The prosecuting attorney, Ralph N. Smith, objected vehemently, but this didn't stop Wirt from proceeding to question Belle about her second husband's death. When Ralph had exhausted his objections, Wirt approached Belle, looked her directly in the eye, and asked when Jennie Olsen was coming home. What exactly did Wirt know? Maybe too much.

Though Ray was found guilty that day, Belle was the one who looked shaken as they left the courthouse. Ray's new employer, farmer John Wheatbrook, paid the fine, and Ray was free again.

It wasn't long before Belle had Ray arrested again for trespassing. Wirt changed his approach during this next trial, and instead of trying to undercut Belle's credibility by referencing the questionable deaths of her former husbands, he provided witnesses who directly challenged Belle's assertions that Ray was prowling about and vandalizing her property. Wirt brought forth two witnesses who swore Ray was at the Wheatbrook farm during the time Belle claimed he was in her farmyard. This time, Ray won. Belle had never been beaten before, and even this small loss was enough to cause her confidence to waver.

But Ray wasn't the only problem she faced.

In another headache for the widow Gunness, neighbors were talking about the sinister happenings at the farm. Mrs. Diesslin told people about a time when she called on Belle, who was sitting near an open window. A strong breeze blew through the window, lifting up the folds of a loose housedress Belle was wearing, revealing a wide belt containing pouches of various sizes and sheaths, which seemed to have been constructed for knives. As far-fetched as that might have sounded at the time, it most likely was true, and little by little, people were beginning to realize it.

One day, she caught Myrtle and Lucy going down the steps to the cellar—a forbidden area—before school. Wanting them to understand the seriousness of their offence, Belle whipped the little girls. They were still crying when they reached the schoolhouse. The teacher asked the girls why they were so upset, and they told her about trying to get into the cellar. Such a story wouldn't take long to spread throughout the small town of La Porte. Belle's treatment of her daughters would also likely bring to mind the daughter who was gone.

When Jennie was sixteen, Belle told everyone that the girl had left to go to school. Most had been told that Jennie was in Los Angeles; others, such as Jennie's family, heard the school was in Minnesota. Now two years later, people were asking why she never came home for a visit. Others, such as Jennie's sisters, her father, her sweetheart, and her friends, wondered why Jennie never answered the letters they sent and why many of them were returned instead.

Jennie was engaged, Belle told people, and would be home for a visit soon. That appeased people for a bit, but she'd have to figure out what to do after the homecoming didn't come to pass.

Swanhild Gunness was another worry. Older now and in hiding after her family saw a strange man skulking around their farm, she was likely able to recall and explain what had happened to her father and her baby sister.

And then there was Asle Helgelien.

As the weeks went by with no word from Andrew, Asle became more and more worried about his brother. Perhaps he had gotten in trouble with the law again. Asle was surprised after reading the letters Belle wrote to Andrew, which were found in his house, that his brother was looking for love. Asle hadn't known about Andrew's reply to the advertisement in the Norwegian newspaper, nor had he known about Andrew's longtime and lengthy correspondences with Belle. Andrew had mentioned a rich Norwegian widow from Indiana in passing, but Asle had never considered the possibility of his brother being in a relationship, much less betrothed. But, at least after having read the letters, he knew where he should start his search.

When Belle began receiving Asle's letters, she assumed she could easily get rid of him with a few carefully constructed lies as she had with all the others who wrote asking about their missing loved ones. On March 27, 1908, she provided Asle with what she thought was a perfectly reasonable response.

Mister Asle K. Helgelien:

I have just received a letter from you wherein you would like to be informed where your brother Andrew is keeping himself. Well, this is exactly what I would also like to know myself, but unfortunately for the moment it is something that is almost impossible for me to give any report on.

She went on to say that Andrew had left La Porte in the middle of January to look for Andrew and Asle's brother who owned a gambling house in Aberdeen. She rambled a bit in a confusing way, maybe to throw Asle off track, writing that when Andrew didn't find his brother he went on to other cities, including Chicago and New York.

"Since then I have neither heard nor seen anything from him," she continued in her letter. "There is a man here who said that he heard he was back in S. Dakota but that was naturally not true. Now this is all I can illuminate of things. I have been waiting each day for some sign from him or that he would come himself, but hereto everything has been in vain, so I will close now with a friendly greeting."

A letter written by Belle to Andrew Helgelien. *Photo courtesy of Ted Hartzell.*

Belle again wrote to Asle on April 11, this time offering several possibilities for Andrew's disappearance, including a "half-crazed" former farmhand.

Mr. A. K. Helgelien:

Your letter I have received some days ago but haven't been able to answer in regard to your brother Andrew. I have tried every which way to find some trace of him. The man who told me he is in South Dakota is named Lamphere, who worked for me for a while. He said he had heard it from someone he knew in Mansfield. I knew right away it was a lie.

But this Lamphere began to find so many wrong things to talk about until at last they took and arrested him, and they had three doctors to examine him and see if he was all right. They found him not quite crazy enough to put in a hospital. But perfectly sane he is not. He is now out under bonds and is going to have a trial next week. Therefore, there is no foundation to the stories Lamphere told. Others have told me that Lamphere was jealous of Andrew and for that reason troubled me this way.

The reason he was looking for his brother, Andrew told me, was that both of them left Aberdeen the same day, and there was some trouble with a man they had found dead there. He said that he had not talked to his brother about it, but had heard it from others and when his brother left home Andrew probably thought this was the reason and that is why he wanted to know if his brother went to Norway alone. Now this is what Andrew told me, and I believe it to be the truth.

Andrew did not say anything to me in regard to the farm or creatures, but I think it would be best for you to sell the farm and creatures as soon as you can and come here in May.

When Andrew comes up there again, which he will no doubt some time, be sure and do not tell him that I told you this or do not tell it to others either. He probably will not like it.

I must now do the best I can here and so we must hope that all will come out all right. I think it is only this half-crazed Lamphere who has started it all, but there is hardly anything to do about it.

Andrew was not very well when he was up here. He had caught a bad cold up there and on his way, so he had quite a cold, but I do not think it anything to talk about. He is otherwise well and strong and I hope nothing has happened to him.

Well, I have done the best I could and given you all the enlightenment I can and if you wish again to write I will gladly answer your respectable letter.

Heartiest regards;
Bella Gunness

On April 24, Belle again wrote to Asle. Several pages long, her letter offers a slightly different story about Andrew's whereabouts, telling Asle that on either January 15 or 16, her fourteen-year-old daughter (her daughters were eleven and nine at the time) took Andrew to the train station so he could visit Michigan City, a town about twelve miles away. She repeats her belief that Andrew was likely hunting for his brother in Chicago, New York, or even Norway.

Belle said she received a letter from Andrew a few days after he left, saying he hadn't yet found his brother. But Belle was quick to say that she no longer had the letter, only a scrap of it, as she believed Ray stole it. She included in the envelope this scrap, which was well worn and without a date or signature, as proof of her sincerity.

Andrew was a dreamer, but Asle was practical and dogged. He continued writing Belle, not put off by her assertions that his brother was in Norway or Chicago or somewhere else. When he discovered that Andrew had emptied out his bank account in Aberdeen, he contacted the First National Bank of La Porte, asking if they had any information about his brother's whereabouts. He received a response from Frank Pitner, the cashier who had waited on Andrew and Belle when they came in on Monday, January 6, 1908, to cash Andrew's bank certificates of deposit.

On April 27, Belle asked Joe to pick up her mail at the post office, which was something she had never done before. He returned with several letters. Belle opened one, and terror spread across her face as she read it. Andrew was coming to La Porte to investigate the disappearance of his brother.

While inside her heart fluttered with anxiety, Belle remained cool and focused enough to develop a plan. She started by calling at the office of her attorney, Melvin E. Leliter, and asking him to draft her will. She needed, she told him, "to prepare for an eventuality. I'm afraid that fool Lamphere is going to kill me and burn my house."

Melvin, who knew Belle well, suggested that if Ray was really such a bother, she should just fill him full of buckshot. After all, Belle was known for pointing her shotgun at people she disagreed with. But that day, Belle was playing the role of a helpless and frightened woman. She sobbed about how worried she was that Ray would bring harm to her and her children.

She instructed Melvin to ensure that her property, both real and personal, went to her three children, Myrtle Adolphine Sorenson, Lucy Bergiant Sorenson, and Philip Alexander Gunness. Not included was her oldest child, Jennie Olsen, whose eighteenth birthday was coming up and who was supposedly on her way home from school.

Belle's will further stated, "In case of the death of any of said children without issue before their death, the survivor is to inherit the whole of the property, and provided also, that in the case of the death of all three of said children without issue, the whole of the property should go to the Norwegian Children's Home."

Melvin asked her if that was the legal name of the home. Belle didn't know for sure, but when the attorney offered to find out and make sure it was correct before she signed the will, Belle told him to write it the way she'd told him. "I don't have time to wait," she said. So Melvin did what she said, and Belle signed the will.

Belle then placed the will in her safe-deposit box and deposited $730 in her savings account. Before going home, she bought a few items, including toys for the kids, cream puffs, and a five-gallon can of kerosene.

That night, Belle, the children, and Joe sat down to a lavish feast. After dinner, Belle handed Joe an orange as a treat and insisted that he eat it right then. Though he didn't really want it after such a large meal, he obliged. They all retired to the parlor and played games. Before long, Joe became so sleepy that he could barely keep his eyes open. He said good night and went to his room, leaving the little family playing with the new toys they got that day.

Even in the face of all these problems, Belle continued business as usual. Her yearning for money and blood, as well as her belief in her own infallibility, made her careless at a time when most would have held back. But she had been so successful for so long even though murder and insurance fraud is a complicated and risky business. Belle engaged in this business on an industrial scale, which demanded an executive management style worthy of the titans who built America's railroads, steel mills, and oil fields—perhaps a comparison to Chicago's slaughterhouses and meat-packing industry would be more fitting. As with those enterprises, the rewards for Belle were great.

Following is a tabulation of the money supposed to have been obtained by Belle through her schemes:

- From Mads Sorenson, her first husband, life insurance: $8,000
- From Peter Gunness, second husband, life insurance: $4,000
- From Charles Erdman, New Castle, Indiana: $5,000
- From Herman Kenitzer, Chicago, Illinois: $5,000
- From fire in Gunness store, insurance: $3,500
- From fire in Gunness house, insurance: $1,500
- From Ole O. Budsberg, Iola, Wisconsin: $2,000
- From John C. Moe, Elbow Lake, Minnesota: $1,500
- From Andrew Helgelien, Aberdeen, South Dakota: $7,000
- From George Berry, Tuscola: $1,500
- From Henry Gurholt, Iola, Wisconsin: $1,000
- From four men, other than those above, whose bodies were found in Belle's graveyard, estimated at $1,000 each: $4,000
- From fifteen other men who were in correspondence with Belle and mysteriously disappeared, estimated at $1,000 each: $15,000

The grand total of $48,300 is equal to about $1,341,627 today. This total doesn't include the insurance money she received for Jennie Gunness, Caroline Sorenson, Axel Sorenson, and any of the foster children she may have insured. Neither does it include Jennie Olsen's legacy nor any money she collected for performing abortions or disposing of bodies for others.

It had been a long and successful run. For years, Belle had exhibited a type of in-your-face insouciance about what she was doing, an "I'm so much smarter than you I can get away with murder" kind of attitude. She and Ray wore victims' coats and watches. Belle accompanied men to the bank, had them withdraw all their money, and then did away with them. People arrived at her farm and never left. Trunks piled up in an empty bedroom, and whole wardrobes of clothes filled her closets. She told different versions of her lies as if she were challenging her audience to call her on it. She even had the audacity to propose that Asle sell Andrew's property and bring the money to La Porte. And yet, no one from her neighborhood, from law enforcement, from the bank, or from La Porte in general seemed able to put the pieces together.

Until Asle came to town.

9

The Fire

THE SHARP ACRID SMELL OF SMOKE SEEPING INTO HIS BED-room and jarring him awake from a deep sleep most likely saved Joseph Maxson's life in the early morning hours of April 28, 1908. Joe jumped out of bed and rushed to the window. Flames were licking up from below. The house was on fire.

Joe had gone to bed early the night before, sleepiness overcoming him around 8:30 while he sat in the parlor as Belle and her three children played games. Belle had insisted he eat an orange earlier in the evening. Authorities would later hypothesize the orange had been poisoned and he wasn't meant to wake at all. However, he did awake earlier in the night to find her standing over him.

Is anybody sick? he asked, and Belle replied no.

I just wanted to see if you were asleep, she said.

When he thought back on that night, he realized she was hiding a hammer in the folds of her skirt.

He'd fallen back to sleep for a second time and woke again when the room began to fill with smoke.

Pulling on his clothes and gum boots, Joe ran to the bedroom door and turned the knob. The door didn't budge. He realized the door was bolted at both the top and bottom on the other side. Joe kicked the door with all his might, but the heavy wood wouldn't give. He had no choice—the only way out of the house was through his second-story window onto the hard ground below.

The Gunness house following the fire. *Photo courtesy of the La Porte County Historical Society.*

Once outside, he didn't stop to clear his smoke-blurred vision but made straight for the shed. By the time he returned with an ax, a neighbor boy, William Clifford, was trying to open the front door. But the door, triple-locked, wouldn't budge. William yelled, "Fire!" but received no response from inside.

Joe pushed William aside, swung the ax hard, and broke through a door panel. Both peered inside but saw nothing but flames. William's father, Michael, and his uncle William Humphrey arrived. When they didn't see anyone from the household outside except for Joe, they asked where the others were and then, when told no one knew, where the bedrooms were located. Joe pointed to several windows on the second floor, and Humphrey threw bricks at them, shattering the glass. The men stared up at the windows to see if anyone poked their head out or if they could hear cries for help. But they only saw flames and heard their crackling as they consumed everything inside.

Joe ran back to the shed, got a ladder, and positioned it under the windows for Humphrey to scale. He peered first in one window and then another—each scene was the same. The beds were empty and looked as if they hadn't been slept in. He tried to see beyond the flames, hoping to spot someone or something that would give a clue as to what had happened to Belle and the three kids, but flames were engulfing the interior, spreading across the floor and walls. The intense heat and thick smoke threatened to overtake him, so he climbed back down.

Michael hurried over to the neighboring Hutson family to sound the alarm. Daniel Hutson hurried over to help while Mrs. Hutson, calm despite her fears, set to making breakfast and coffee for the stricken Gunness family. They'd be hungry, she figured, after all this.

It had only taken a few moments for Michael and Daniel to appear on the scene, but by now the house was a solid blaze. Other neighbors were awake and reacting to the red glow on the horizon. Soon, there were several people milling about the yard, unable to do anything but watch the flames consume the great house. The heat held them back in a wide arc around the house.

Daniel patted Joe on the shoulder and told him to inform the sheriff. Joe had difficulty pulling his eyes away from the ruin in front of him, but a cracking beam sounded like a shot and startled him to action.

The panicked horses were nickering and pacing in the barn, and it took four men to get the buggy horse calmed enough to hitch up. Joe struggled to get the horse on the road, and it wasn't until five o'clock in the morning when he knocked on Sheriff Albert Smutzer's door.

Though Albert had been sleeping and was yawning as he opened the door, he reacted quickly at hearing the word *fire*. In a matter of minutes, he was dressed and on the road in his red Ford runabout with Deputy Sheriff William Antiss at his side. Joe followed in the horse and buggy, far behind the much faster sporty car that Albert had somehow managed to buy on a sheriff's salary.

By the time Joe turned the horse back onto Belle's property, Albert had organized the busy scene. Neighbors from near and far had come to help, and the fire company had also arrived. A water brigade had been set up, and lines of people formed, filling pails of water and passing them down until they reached those standing nearest the fire, who threw the water on the flames. Then the pails were handed back, making their way from person to person until they were filled once more at the end. Though the process was repeated again and again, it had little effect as the flames continued to dance and leap as they engulfed the home.

Crowds gather at the Gunness farm after the fire. *Photo courtesy of the La Porte County Historical Society.*

Finally by noon, the flames had subsided—there was little left to burn. In its place was a jumble of debris, piles of hot ash, burning hot bricks, and the remains of the stone cellar. What had been a beautiful and spacious brick home was now in ruins.

Talk buzzed among the onlookers, and a rumor spread that Belle and her family had escaped and made it to nearby Michigan City, though no one asked why she would take the kids and go there rather than stay and help put out the fire. It was more hope than anything and quickly quashed. The breakfast that Mrs. Hutson had prepared for the Gunness family was eaten by those trying to put out the fire.

There were, of course, many questions. The most important, besides whether the Gunness family had survived, was how the fire started. The answer to that soon became apparent.

Daniel Hutson heard a group of people talking about the smell of a queer smoke, and he too thought it was different from other fires. Instead of burning lumber, he thought, the smell was that of rags, and it was really pronounced when standing near a pine tree on the north side of the house.

There was a reason for that as searchers soon discovered. The queer smell was kerosene, and someone had poured a great quantity of it in the north corner of the cellar near the door and then set the flammable liquid on fire. As word passed through the crowd

Workers sifting the debris looking for the missing head. *Photo courtesy of the Steve Shook Collection.*

about the find, people said wisely to each other, No wonder the fire was so intense.

Some great malice was at play here; kerosene meant arson. That must mean someone had wanted the widow and her children dead. Who would do something so horrendous, some asked, but the sheriff and a majority of onlookers had already settled on an answer: Ray Lamphere. After all, Belle had been fervently informing anyone who would listen that Ray was a threat to her and her family and that he had explicitly threatened to burn her house down. Who else could possibly be to blame? For those on the scene, no longer was Ray just a jilted lover and fired employee. Now, he was an arsonist and quadruple murderer.

Albert figured Ray likely ran after setting the fire, but he sent Deputy Anstiss and Deputy Leroy Marr to find the farmhand to cover his bases, then continued to oversee what now was a crime scene. The two deputy sheriffs drove to the house of John Wheatbrook, where Ray worked. On their way up the drive, the police vehicle got stuck in the mud, and so while Anstiss remained in the auto, Marr trudged up to the farmhouse and knocked on the door.

"Did they get the woman and three children out of that house?" Ray asked when he opened the door and recognized the deputy sheriff. It was, the deputy thought, an admission of guilt.

Ray kept jabbering away—but that was so characteristic of Ray. Without the deputy asking, he spewed forth all sorts of information. He was innocent, he said, and had an alibi—he'd spent the previous night at the home of Liz Smith. He said he arose about 4 a.m., and as he walked from Liz's to the Wheatbrook farm, he saw smoke coming from Belle's house. But unlike all the others who had rushed over to the farm to help, Ray, according to his own statement, had just kept walking.

The search continued at the farm but not for survivors. Everyone there understood the grim truth. They were looking for the bodies of a mother and her young children.

Most of the volunteers had toiled from before dawn, but though it was mid-afternoon, they didn't stop. They were utterly exhausted but driven by the bonds of a community to take care of their own. Some of the watchers stayed, while others had chores they needed to do. But all had moved freely around the farm. Who knows how much evidence was lost?

Four more tedious hours went by and still no bodies. All who had stayed were cold, wet, and tired—their quest seemingly endless.

William Humphrey, one of the first on the scene, was directed to dig in the last unexplored cellar corner. Though sweating and exhausted, he was determined to finish the job and stuck his shovel into the ground for what seemed the millionth time. This time, it hit something soft. He was quiet for a moment, not quite believing it possible. "Here they are," he said simply. He called over the sheriff, and together they carefully dug out the spot.

Putting up their shovels, the searchers crowded around as ashes were gently brushed from the body, and the burned face of a girl appeared. Soon they'd uncovered a second girl, and then close by was the body of a woman holding a young child cradled close to her chest—presumably, Belle and her young son. A big sigh of relief—they were found.

And then horror struck as more ashes and debris were swept away. Lucy had a hole in her forehead. Philip's mouth was open, and his legs were gone at the knees. Bones protruded through the flesh of all three children, and in several places, it was burned completely away. But nothing was quite as shocking as the state of the woman. She didn't have a head.

Picking up their brooms and shovels, the onlookers began searching again. But finally, they called it quits. The head would have to wait for another day.

Once he arrived at the jail, Ray again insisted on his innocence. Neither the sheriff nor the deputies believed him. Reporters came to the jail, wanting to talk to Ray. He was, of course, willing to talk, but Albert didn't let them in.

But there was one person they couldn't keep out. Liz Smith, fiery as ever, marched into the jail. She had come to provide an alibi.

"That man Lamphere came to my house Monday night and asked for a room. He said he was sick and had no money," she told the sheriff. "'If I ever get any money I'll pay you,' he told me, and then he sat down for a while. Then he woke up and said, 'Are you going to let me have a room?' I told him I thought so, and he went over to Smiths saloon and got something to eat.

"I had my alarm clock set for 4:30, and he turned it back to 3:30. I heard the alarm go off and went in to wake him up. He was snoring like a good fellow, and I told him it was after four o'clock. He said, 'My God I ought to be over to Wheatbrook's by this time,' and started out."

It wasn't the first time Liz had tried to help Ray out, and it wouldn't be the last. But this time, Liz's corroboration did little to convince the authorities of Ray's innocence. Albert had already decided Ray was guilty, and he was going to do everything he could to send him to the gallows.

Interrogations continued, but Ray refused to confess to the crime. Frustrated, Sheriff Smutzer ushered Ray down to the morgue, where he was forced to look at the remains of the family he had worked alongside and spent so many cozy evenings with. Ray put a hand to his mouth and turned away from the charred bodies.

Still, Ray did not confess.

Albert took Ray to court for his arraignment, where the charges were read: "One Ray Lamphere did then and there unlawfully and feloniously kill and murder one Belle Gunness in the perpetration of arson and did then and there feloniously, willfully, and maliciously set fire to the house of the said Belle Gunness." Ray pled not guilty to these charges and was returned to the jail to be held without bond. The grand jury was set to meet on May 11.

As Ray languished in his cell, the outside world was aswirl with speculation and stories, and before long, word of the event was carried across state lines. Newspapers picked up the story the day after the fire, and in this way, word reached Nellie, Belle's sister, in Chicago. Granted, it had been several years since Nellie had seen her sister, but Nellie was taken aback by the account of Belle's will. That Belle's sizeable estate should go to the Norwegian Children's Home of Chicago rather than her living relatives perplexed Nellie, and she meant to contest the will after seeing her sister laid to rest.

Nellie and her son, John, boarded a train to La Porte that Friday and immediately upon arriving went to the morgue. She couldn't bring herself to look at her sister's gruesome remains and asked her son to do so in her stead. He did, saying he was pretty sure they were those of his aunt Belle. The bodies would have to be autopsied, but following that, Nellie made arrangements to have the bodies transported to Chicago, where she would see them interred in Forest Home Cemetery, where Mads, Caroline, Axel, and Jennie Gunness, Belle's stepdaughter, lay at rest.

Also arriving by train from Chicago was May Olander, Jennie Olsen's older sister. She had read about the tragedy in the paper and was relieved not to see Jennie's name. Belle had told everyone that Jennie was on her way home for a visit. Had she been in the house when the house caught on fire? Could her body still be hidden under the rubble? May thought she knew the answer to that given how Belle had tried to isolate Jennie from her family and how she had lied about the death of Peter Gunness.

No one knew where Jennie was. Indeed, no one knew whether Jennie was in school in California or Minnesota. But May noticed something that everyone else had missed, including Belle's attorney. The will stipulated that Belle's money should go to her three children—Myrtle, Lucy, and Philip. There was no mention of Jennie Olsen. Did Belle mean to cut her out of the will, or did it mean Jennie was already dead? There were still so many things to know, more than anyone could even begin to envision.

The man who had inadvertently started the fall of Belle's house of cards was on his way to La Porte.

10

The Discovery

AFTER THE FIRE, WHILE THE RUBBLE WAS STILL SMOKING and Joe Maxson and Daniel Hutson were continuing to dig through the debris in what was left of the basement looking for Belle's head, Asle Helgelien rode the train into town. This wasn't a spur-of-the-moment decision. Asle believed Belle was lying and had sent a letter to say he was coming to La Porte. But before he could make plans for the upkeep of two farms while he was gone, a letter arrived from Frank Pitner of the La Porte National Bank. Inside the envelope, along with a note, were newspaper clippings about the fire. Not long after receiving them, Asle hurriedly headed east.

After disembarking at the depot at midnight, Sunday, May 3, after almost two days on the train, Asle spent his first night in La Porte at the Teegarden Hotel. The next morning, he stopped at the office of the *La Porte Herald*, purchased all the papers from the day of the fire up until that day, and then hurriedly walked to the courthouse. In one of her letters, Belle had written that she had used some of Andrew's money in exchange for giving him a part mortgage on her farm. But there was no mortgage on file. He also stopped at the bank to talk in person to the clerk who had sent him the news clippings. And then he headed to his next planned stop.

"I went to the sheriff," Asle testified. "I had made up my mind that my brother must be in La Porte. I showed the sheriff my

Asle Helgelien. *Photo courtesy of the La Porte County Historical Society.*

introduction from the sheriff in Aberdeen. We spent the afternoon, Sheriff Smutzer and I, talking over the situation."

Overall, Albert Smutzer was polite to this poorly dressed man but was uninterested in Asle's theory that Belle had a part in his brother's disappearance. It was not an unusual stance for the sheriff to take. When he met with Gustav Gunness, who believed Belle murdered his brother Peter, Albert refused to investigate further despite the evidence Gustav presented to him. He had done the same with other families looking for loved ones.

To give the sheriff his due, at the time, his office was inundated with calls and letters from people who had sighted Belle, claimed to know something about the case, or offered weird theories. One insurance agent said he had tried to stop by Belle's farm several times to see her, but his horse, frightened when he tried to turn it onto her property, refused to move. He'd been saved by a clairvoyant horse.

Albert, sensing Asle's doggedness and determination—after all he had traveled all the way from South Dakota to La Porte during planting season—tried to be somewhat helpful. He drove Asle to Swan Nicholson's house so he could spend the night, figuring the Scandinavians would get along. The Nicholsons, who were Belle's neighbors, had once been friendly with the widow, but, as might be expected, ongoing incidents about trespassing cows and Belle threatening them with her shotgun had soured the relationship. Swan Nicholson and his son Albert had also been at Belle's home the night Peter Gunness was done in by the meat grinder and suspected that he had been murdered. Mrs. Nicholson and her son told Asle they had noticed a man driving back and forth in the horse and buggy with Mrs. Gunness to and from town during the first part of January. That man was most likely Andrew. After that, they hadn't seen him again. And no, they hadn't seen him going to the train depot either. He had just disappeared. That wasn't unusual, of course. People disappeared from the Gunness home on a regular basis. And they never said goodbye.

From the Nicholson home, Asle walked over to the Gunness place and spent the rest of the day working with Joe and Daniel digging through the debris in the cellar. The two men described how jealous Ray had been of Andrew, whom he called "the big Swede." But as to Andrew's whereabouts, they had no idea. Giving up for the evening, Asle returned to the Nicholsons, where he planned to spend the night and then catch the train home the next day.

But in the morning, he still felt unsettled, experiencing an overwhelming need to return to the farm again. Belle's fruit trees were starting to blossom, and their beauty and fragrance were at odds with the ruined house and outbuildings, the twisted pipes, and

Postcard with stars marking the spots where bodies were discovered at the Gunness farm. *Photo courtesy of the Steve Shook Collection.*

the exposed basement filled with crumbled bricks, plaster, and the charred remains of household items. Joe and Daniel were there again, sifting through the rubble.

Asle had come to the unwelcome realization that Andrew most likely was dead and buried on the property. But there were forty-three acres, and he didn't know where to begin looking. He walked all around the farm and the grounds of the house looking for something odd or unusual that might be a clue to Andrew's where-abouts. Discouraged, he talked to Joe and Daniel again, asking a few more questions. Had there been any holes in the ice on the lake that winter? How deep was the lake? If he could just find the right question to ask, he thought, then maybe he could come up with the right answer as to what happened to his brother.

Joe and Daniel tried but couldn't help. Even more discouraged and feeling an overwhelming sense of defeat, Asle began walking back to the Nicholson home, where he'd grab his belongings and head to the train depot. But those nagging thoughts of something undone didn't let up. Andrew was here, and it was up to Asle to find him. He couldn't fail the brother he loved.

"I told the boys goodbye," he would say at the coroner's inquest. "When I had come down into the road I was not satisfied, and I went back again. I went to the cellar and asked [Joe] Maxson whether he knew of any hole or dirt being digger [*sic*] up there, about the place, early in the spring. He told me he filled up a hole in the garden there in March. He did not remember the date. Mrs. Gunness had told him she had had the hole dug to put rubbish in.

"Mrs. Gunness herself helped, raking, picking up old cans, shoes or rubbish, and the man, Maxson, I think, wheeled it in the wheelbarrow to the hole and dumped it in. After putting in the rubbish, they covered it with dirt. I got Maxson to show me the hole, and we all three of us started to dig."

A short time after they began to dig, Asle noticed "an awful bad smell."

Joe said that Belle had thrown in a lot of tomato and fish cans and maybe that was why it smelled. But the stench, thought Asle, was much worse than just household garbage.

He was right.

A few feet down, Joe's shovel struck something covered with a gunnysack.

"We lifted the oil cloth and the gunnysack," said Asle. "Then we saw the neck of a body and an arm."

Get the sheriff, said Asle, and for the second time in less than a week, Joe hitched the horse to Belle's buggy and headed down the road toward town.

Asle covered their find with an old coat and several gunnysacks that lay scattered about the grounds, and then he and Daniel cleared away the dirt, digging around the hole until Albert, accompanied by La Porte County Coroner Charles S. Mack, arrived. The sheriff grabbed a shovel, and the men continued digging. Soon, they'd uncovered a putrid stew of human remains turned partially to a jelly-like ooze of severed arms, legs cut from about three inches above the knee, fingers hacked off at the joints, and a decapitated head with all its teeth remaining except a missing second right upper molar.

Despite the condition of the skull—the flesh had rotted away, and the eye sockets were empty dark holes—Asle recognized what they had uncovered. They were looking at his brother's face.

"I recognize it by the form of the face—across the eye, the forehead, across the cheeks," he would tell the judge and jury later.

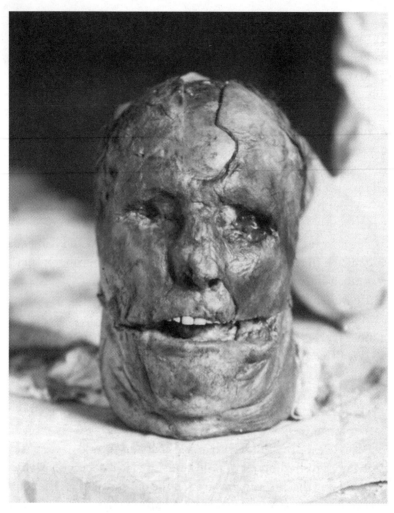

The severed head of Andrew Helgelien. *Photo courtesy of the La Porte County Historical Society.*

"When you have been with your brother every day for fifteen years, you know him."

As the four men studied the body parts, a thought passed between them. What was left of Andrew's clothing showed no trace of blood. Could Andrew have been bled out, maybe strung up so his blood dripped into a vat? And if so, why, and even worse, was he alive at the time?

Andrew Helgelien's mug shot. *Photo courtesy of the La Porte County Historical Society.*

A Bertillon expert, so called because he was trained in the techniques of Alphonse Bertillon, considered one of the forefathers of modern forensics, was summoned. He used measurements taken from when Andrew was in prison and confirmed Asle's identification.

Later, an autopsy revealed that whoever had dissected Andrew had done so with surgical precision. This was no hatchet job, but the work of a very competent individual equipped with extremely sharp knives. Belle's knife skills were well known to her neighbors who had watched her butcher hogs before curing and smoking the meat. Did she learn her techniques from Peter Gunness, who had worked as a butcher? Or was it just so much practice?

Dr. J. H. William Meyer, a coroner at Cook County Hospitals who oversaw Andrew's postmortem exam, remarked on how well preserved his organs were. "They are in such a condition as we find in a man who had been dead only two or three days," he said, noting that it was most likely that the poison found in his body had acted as a preservative. He made another discovery that brought some solace to Asle.

Andrew, a husky two-hundred-pound man who lived the hard life of a farmer, had fought valiantly for his life. Despite the fatal amounts of strychnine and arsenic found in his stomach, there were two deep cuts, open to the bone, in his left wrist, most likely from fighting off an attacker with a knife. His fist, which was closed when pulled from his grave, revealed a hunk of short curly brown hair. It was a small victory of sorts. But no one knew who the hair belonged to—it matched neither Ray's nor Belle's. It might have belonged to Julius Truelson, but no one ever tried to see if it matched.

When Asle testified during Ray's trial, he described how Belle's letters created an overwhelming pull on his lonely brother, whom he described as "something of a mystic."

"He lived too much in imagination for a farmer in Dakota," he said. "He could not forget the fjords and mountains of his nativity. When the Gunness woman began to write him letters, he was fascinated. She was a clever woman. She wrote of the things he loved. She discussed Norwegian places and Norwegian ways, and she told him she loved him, and he believed her, because the poor fellow was in that mood where he would have renounced richness in America for a crust at home. The widow held him spellbound. He loved her for her letters. Of her personality he had doubts. I know that, but still he could not believe she was as he had been told. So, he went to his death."

11

Bringing Up Bodies

ON THAT SPRING DAY, AFTER ASLE FOUND HIS BROTHER, THE five men stood surveying the surrounding fields and farmyard, noting the many areas where the ground had slightly caved in. Known as soft spots by forensic scientists, these were indications that decaying matter underneath—such as cadavers—had rotted away. There were more bodies out there, they realized.

The sheriff asked Joe to point out other places where holes had been dug, and he led the men to a spot in the hog pen's fence corner. They began to dig, hoping against hope that they would find nothing but trash. And they did find trash, quite a bit—tin cans, broken crockery, toys, a lamp. The sheriff insisted they keep digging.

About four feet down, the rubbish pile ended, exposing an accumulation of human bones. One of the men removed an old dishpan and found a skull with long blond tresses beneath. They recognized this at once as belonging to Jennie Olsen. The date was May 5, 1908, what would have been her eighteenth birthday.

They set up a makeshift morgue in the shed, and after the grave had been excavated and the jumble of bones laid out, they determined that the heads, torsos, arms, and legs made up four bodies: two men, one woman, and one female adolescent, Jennie. The men, dirty and soul-weary, left the farm for the day; it had just been too much to bear. While the others sought the comfort of their loved

The family-owned Cutler Funeral Home, still in business, used white horses to pull the morgue carriages carrying the female victims and used black horses for the men. *Photo courtesy of the La Porte County Historical Society.*

ones, Sheriff Smutzer marched to the jail and confronted Ray with the discovery.

"Five bodies! That woman! I knew she was bad, but this is awful!" Ray exclaimed.

He denied having any knowledge of the murders but admitted to having his suspicions. He said that in the past Belle had asked him to buy rat poison and chloroform. He also recounted the arrival of a man with a black mustache whom Belle claimed was a friend of Jennie's. He had brought a large trunk with him, but the trunk remained at the house even after Belle said he had gone away.

The case quickly spiraled into an even more chilling and complex scenario when further digging commenced the following day. The farmyard soon became known as Belle's Cemetery as more corpses—men, women, and children—were brought to the surface.

Local photographer William Koch had the good luck of being outside Cutler's Funeral Home as the horse-pulled corpse wagon pulled out into the street and headed toward the Gunness farm.

Gunness Stew served in local restaurants and fooling around at the scene were among the many lighthearted ways people treated the murders. *Photo courtesy of the La Porte County Historical Society.*

Despite the cold rain, Koch followed the wagon on his bike with camera in hand.

Photographers like Koch recorded the scenes unfolding over the upcoming days, preserving the horror into the next century. Gruesome, the images, which are on display at the La Porte County Historical Society, show open graves filled with badly decomposed bodies, teeth, torsos, legs, and arms. Body parts were everywhere—in the pigpen, among the ruin of the barn, on a hillside. We see Andrew's face as it was when Asle, Albert, Coroner Mack, Joe, and Daniel first removed it from the grave. It's easy to overuse "nightmarish," but in this case, it was that and more. Belle had made butchery into a science. Armed with poisons, carving knives and saws, gunnysacks, and quicklime, she became an assembly line of death.

Quicklime, a chemical compound known as calcium oxide, accelerates the decomposition process, three months of the chemical compound equaling ten years of nature's work. Quicklime was used in medieval times to help stop the spread of the plague, and the Nazis spread a thick layer of quicklime on the floor of cattle cars before forcing Jews and other victims aboard.

Adding to the surreal quality, the farm quickly became a tourist attraction. Black-and-white images show sightseers dressed in their weekend best—women in long skirts with heels and stylish hats; men dressed in overcoats and wearing fedoras, cap hats, homburgs, and derbies; young girls in dresses; and boys in suits—walking through mud and dirt. They were, of course, trampling and destroying evidence. There were exceptions though. One young boy discovered a human leg bone and turned it over to the police.

Newspapers reported all the gory details and sold plenty of copies.

"The bones had been crushed on the ends, as though they had been . . . struck with hammers after they were dismembered. Quicklime had been scattered over the faces and stuffed in the ears," reported the *Chicago Inter Ocean*.

The *La Porte Weekly Herald* reported, "All the Gunness victims were buried in quicklime, it has been noticed. This was for the purpose of aiding disintegration. It was discovered yesterday afternoon that Mrs. Gunness bought considerable quicklime of Moore & Richter, saying she used it for building purposes and for disinfecting purposes. Heavy sacks she purchased of Wesley Fogle."

The *Indianapolis Star* reported:

Corpses and skeletons, rotting bundles of human flesh, all that is left of the many victims of multi-murderess Belle Gunness, today offered mute reproach of the ribald gayety of hundreds of excursionists who came from far and near to hold a monster picnic in a graveyard.

With the mellow sun of an early Indian summer day beaming down upon them, the throngs gathered around the ghastly corpses. Passing over the fated ground which must have been the scene of many a tragedy and midnight burial, the excursionists told and retold the stories of the female fiend's work, but even in telling there was lost much of the tragic and something akin to holiday atmosphere prevailed.

The crowds kept coming. The *La Porte Weekly Herald* reported in their May 14, 1908 edition that the interurban increased its schedule and added extra cars to accommodate the crowds which were estimated to be 10,000 to 15,000 on one day alone.

They inspected the holes from which were taken skeletons and decomposed bodies, looked over the edges of the brick walls into the cellar, poked their faces against the window of the carriage house, where lay nine of the skeletons and surmised on the possibility

Joe Maxon and Sheriff Smutzer digging for corpses. *Photo courtesy of the Steve Shook Collection.*

of Mrs. Gunness being dead or alive. . . . It was a great day for the morbid curiosity seekers not only at La Porte and vicinity but of all the nearby cities, towns and hamlets and some cities one to two hundred miles away.

The first Lake Shore train arrived at 5:10 in the morning, carrying 75 people. The largest crowd on a single train arrived from the east, its nine cars packed to the doors. Two morning trains from Chicago were filled to overflowing while over 500 passengers from Indianapolis and points in between riding on the Lake Erie railroad pulled into the station at noon. The Pere Marquette railroad ran a special train picking up crowds at every station until, at Wellsboro, the cars were so full no other passengers could board. Since no other passenger cars were available to add to the train, a string of freight cars was coupled on and used to haul the overflow. Even small airplanes, still a very new mode of transportation, were used to get people to the farm. Passengers arriving by train (or plane) needed to get out to the farm and the paper said every livery rig in town was out while carryalls and wagonettes did a rushing business between the corner of Main Street and Michigan Avenue and the Gunness home from early morning until late at night. McClung Road, typically a quiet country lane, was clogged with automobiles, pedestrians and carriages.

They were still digging up bodies when local restaurants started serving such "delicacies" as Gunness stew. Maybe the reality was

Some of those in attendance at the auction. *Photo courtesy of the La Porte County Historical Society.*

such that it was easier to make jokes about it than to focus on the carnage and loss.

Indeed, the horror of it was reduced to postcards showing the destruction such as the one sent to Ms. J. L. Elliott of Springfield, Illinois, with the following message: "Dear Sister, I received postal and pepper thanks for same this is a view of Mrs. Gunness' home after the fire & suppose you have read all about it in the papers."

Another reads, "The pony on this card is the one that was sold at the auction. They are going to stop digging over there today as they say they have all the bodys."

An auction was held on May 29, 1908, with approximately five thousand people in attendance bidding extraordinary amounts for everyday items. More than five hundred carriages were tied about the farm. Most items sold at five to ten times their ordinary sale value. The three items attracting the greatest attention at the sale were Belle's pony, the pony cart, and a shepherd dog. The dog sold for $107.

Joe Maxson made money by traveling around with a display of artifacts and photos from the farm.

Some reporters wrote eighty thousand to one hundred thousand words to file with papers back home. The Chicago papers covered it as did New York papers. It didn't matter whether the newspaper

The Gunness family dog and buggy, which were sold at the auction.
Photo courtesy of the La Porte County Historical Society.

was small or large, all published lengthy stories because everyone wanted to read about the grisly murders. So many rumors and false leads abounded that at least in one case, two stories running on the same day in the same paper contradicted each other.

As more bodies surfaced, Belle's image began to morph from heroic mom who sheltered her young son while facing advancing flames into a monster mom, and her fate—death by fire or life on the lam—was a nationwide discussion point.

The prosecution and the police, including Albert, held that Belle was dead, heartlessly killed by Ray. Luckily for the perennially unlucky handyman, he had Wirt Worden as his attorney. Wirt, a heartbreaker among many of the females in town, had sat, along with his secretary, Bessie Folant, all day in the rain while searchers dug through rubble looking for Belle and the children on that first day after the fire. He also offered a reward to anyone providing information on Belle's location. It's unlikely Ray could pay him much, if anything at all, but that didn't keep Wirt from being zealous in his defense.

No one knows exactly how many people were buried on the farm. Some graves had more feet than arms; some bodies were missing heads. It was probably a brilliant strategy on Belle's part

Joe Maxon, the only survivor of the fire, took the Belle show on the road with a makeshift booth that he could easily set up for shows. *Photo courtesy of the Steve Shook Collection.*

as it made identifying all the remains impossible. Bodies were being dug up so quickly that no one really took the time to sort them by putting all the right hands in one container, all the left hands in another.

The coroner kept churning out reports. While many questioned whether the woman's body found in the remains of the Gunness house was in fact Belle, there was no question about the identities of the children. The coroner's inquisitions included the location and manner of the bodies' discoveries, statements from witnesses, autopsy results, and the conclusions of the coroner. Following are excerpts from the coroner's inquisition of the body of Philip Gunness.

Coroner's Inquisition

I, the undersigned, coroner of the County of La Porte and state of Indiana, by virtue of my office empowered to inquire, and report on such matters, now report:

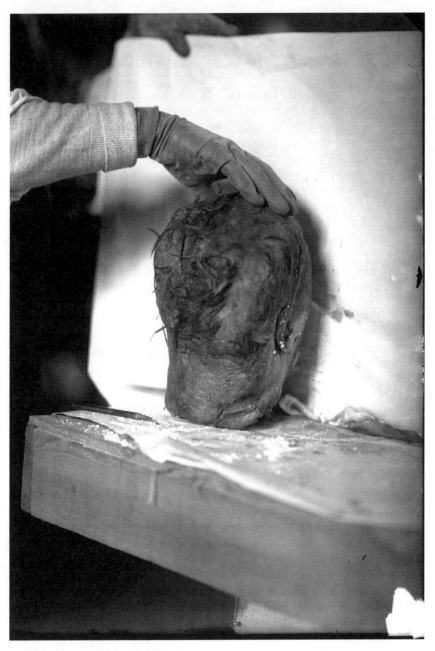

The back of a victim's head. *Photo courtesy of the La Porte County Historical Society.*

That as soon as notified and on the 28th day of April 1908, and from day to day thereafter proceeded to inquire upon view of the body, a description of which is hereto attached marked Exhibit "A," how and in what manner said person came to his death.

After having examined said body, I heard evidence as provided by law, and also caused a postmortem examination of said body to or made by Dr. J.H. Wm. Meyer.

The following named witnesses gave evidence, to wit: Joseph Maxson, William Clifford, William Humphrey, Michael Clifford, Daniel M Hutson, and J.H. William Meyer, M.D., and their respective depositions subscribed by them are hereto attached, made a part hereof and marked respectively as Exhibits "B," "C," "D," etc.

It is my verdict that the body so viewed is that of Philip Alexander Gunness; that he came to his death through felonious homicide, and that the perpetrator thereof is to me unknown.

Exhibit "G"

Dr. J.H. Wm. Meyer being duly sworn deposes as follows:

At the order of Charles S. Mack coroner of La Porte County, Indiana, I performed an autopsy on May 4th, 1908, upon the remains of a male child found in the ruins of Mrs. Belle Gunness' house and brought to the Cutler Morgue. The body has been burned very severely. The legs burned off at the knees and [illegible] missing frontal bone burned through exposing the brain. Posterior three-fourths of cranium remained intact. Hair covers the occipital region. Remains of skull showed no fracture or penetrating wound. Length of remains 4 feet 7 inches.

Body was most burned on back, spinal column being exposed full length and vertebrae charred.

Lungs found collapsed pericardium could be recognized. Head found in systole all cavities empty. There was a large hemorrhage into the pericardium. Stomach empty. Litigated stomach at both openings and removed it. For purpose of identification the ligatures of the two ends are tied together and given in charge of the coroner. Bladder empty; both arms burned off. Testicle in position. From the condition of the body it is not possible to determine the cause of death.

J.M. Wm. Meyer

Subscribed and sworn to be before me this 12th day of May 1908.

Chas. S. Mack, coroner

During the autopsy performed by Dr. Meyer, Jennie Olsen's age was determined by her wisdom teeth, which had perforated the bone but had likely not come through the gums. She was missing teeth and had several very large cavities. Her long blond hair remained on the scalp. The trunk of her body was in an advanced state of disintegration, wrote the coroner, so that it was impossible to determine if the head and trunk belonged together. Externally, the sex of the body couldn't be determined, though upon opening her abdomen, Dr. Meyer located her uterus, which was of natural size and easily distinguishable from the rest of the putrefied mass.

The number of dead seemed endless, and then suddenly, while there were still many more acres to explore, Sheriff Smutzer shut down the recovery without saying why exactly. The digging stopped despite many soft spots remaining. Sheriff Smutzer formally announced the termination of the Belle Gunness investigation on June 5, 1928, two months from its start. He believed that Belle was dead, that all the bodies of her victims had been recovered, "and that the man who caused the fire which destroyed the home is in custody with sufficient evidence to convict him."

Those who are at all familiar with mysteries and crime scene investigation can easily point out numerous errors regarding the way the Gunness case was handled, starting from the beginning when hordes of sightseers—sometimes fifteen thousand in one day—were allowed to traverse the crime scene. The reason for this negligence is unclear. It could have been due to sheer ignorance about preserving evidence. Or could it be that the sightseers were used as a way to obliterate any remaining clues? The second mistake, Fishtrap Lake—the perfect place to dump bodies—was never dragged. Asle Helgelien himself wondered if his brother's corpse had been dumped in the untouched lake—so dragging it should have been part of the investigation. Third, the recent slab of concrete Belle had laid remained intact, not to mention all of the remaining soft spots on the property that were not investigated. The public questioned why Sheriff Smutzer did not break open the cement. "It is to be hoped for Indiana's sake, if not for La Porte's, that the last has been heard of the Gunness [case], unless Sheriff

Smutzer decides to dig up that cement floor," was part of a rather sarcastic editorial in the *Hammond Times*.

Though a new house has been built on the grounds of Belle's farm, the bodies of the missing most likely still remain. Maybe when they're found, if they are, with all the new forensic innovations available now that weren't available before, we'll know about the victims—who they were and how they died. They are probably waiting for just that.

12

The Confession

THE SPADES UNEARTHED A VARIETY OF ITEMS AS INVESTIGA-
tors searched for the missing head. The list was long: boots, the
clasp of a woman's purse, the metal frame of a pocketbook, fragments of clothing, several initialed rings, and so on. The rings were
from much happier days—one was the engagement ring Peter
Gunness gave to his first wife; the other two were wedding rings
the couple exchanged on their wedding day. Other pieces of jewelry were also dug up, including a plethora of watches and watch
cases. But no discovery created as much mystery as several pieces
of jewelry inscribed with the name and address of Mae O'Reilly of
Rochester, New York. As soon as they surfaced, La Porte authorities contacted the Rochester police, who in turn went in search of
a woman by that name.

There was a Mae O'Reilly, and she had plenty of relatives in
Rochester. But as for Mae herself, she didn't live there anymore.

Then a packet arrived at the sheriff's office in La Porte. The
return address was Vernon, Texas, the sender a man who identified
himself as Julius Truelson. The enclosed document was a lengthy
confession of helping Belle commit her crimes. Julius recounted
many horrors as well as the devil-like deal he'd made with Belle.

Married in 1905, Truelson soon deserted his new wife, got
arrested several times, and served a short sentence at the Elmira,
New York, reformatory. There, according to records, he'd been an

exemplary prisoner, showing exceptional brightness and diligence in the courses he took there. But imprisonment hadn't convinced him to change his ways. He decided to end his marriage, but instead of divorce, he wanted her dead. So after his release, Julius located his wife and convinced her to go with him to La Porte.

Belle had agreed to get rid of Mrs. Truelson but only if Julius buried her body afterward. Not a pleasant task for any husband, no matter how alienated he was from his former loved one, and Julius really wasn't emotionally up to the task. But that was the deal.

Julius arrived at Belle's home, accompanied by his wife, Mae O'Reilly from Rochester, New York. One might think this proved Mae O'Reilly was dead. But like so much of this case, what looked to be simple wasn't.

"What I have to say and confess in the following paragraphs, I hope will be withheld from the press, as my parents are a respected family, and let me say I can withhold my guilt no longer and by turning state's evidence I hope leniency will be shown me," Julius wrote in his confession. He was so eager to get the confession to the authorities in La Porte that he wrote it up three times, begged the judge to send one copy, and just to be sure it reached the right people, somehow smuggled another copy out of jail to be mailed to La Porte.

"I have been an accomplice in crime with Mrs. Belle Gunness in La Porte. I have just learned she and her three children are dead and Lamphere, another accomplice, is under arrest. Being equally guilty with Lamphere, I am man enough to take my medicine with him. I will be brief for I don't believe in putting too much in writing, so we'll just stay with the affairs I had in the matter.

"On June 21st, 1907, I brought my first victim to her place, a Mae F. O'Reilly of Rochester, whom I married and wanted to get rid of, and later a Frank X. Reidinger of Delafield, Wisconsin, who she roped in by her ads. This was a month later, in July, I think. Lamphere and I buried these bodies in the same place, near the railroad tracks in the rear of the farm. After this, I went East and lay low, in the home of my parents."

Mae was living in Rochester, New York, when she met Julius. It was a quick courtship, and the two married a day later at St. Peter's Church in Albany, New York, on August 4, 1905. They honeymooned at the Powers Hotel in Rochester. But it was to be a brief honeymoon. Julius deserted his bride to join the Navy and then almost immediately went AWOL. Discharged for desertion, he was arrested for forging checks, joined the Army, deserted again, and ended up being sent to Elmira.

During their time apart, neither Julius nor Mae bothered to file for divorce, though both married again.

According to Mae's relatives when questioned by authorities, she had left Rochester following the brutal murder of Florence McFarlane (also spelled McFarland and McFarlin), her best friend and fellow coworker at the Bell Telephone Company. The murderer was Lulu Youngs, who also worked with them. Lulu, it seems, had strong objections with her husband's ongoing infatuation with McFarlane. Mae was supposed to testify in the grand jury and trial but did not show up for either.

At the time of Florence's murder, we get a very close-up view of Mae in an interview she gave to a young reporter who found her to be very pretty and flirtatious but ultimately able to obfuscate any knowledge she had of the brutal death of her young friend. Indeed, during the in-depth interview full of quotes from Mae and observations of her movements, one doesn't get the idea of a grieving friend. It is also intriguing that she didn't testify but instead left town. Did Mae know more about Lulu Youngs, who stabbed Florence multiple times as her husband's mistress fled from room to room in the handsome home where she lived, finally dying in the arms of a woman she considered to be like a grandmother?

Her uncle by marriage, John Doyle, a bartender at a Rochester tavern, said she'd left town because she didn't want to be associated with the murder and was now living in New York City. No, he didn't have an address for her. How did he know she was in New York? Because one of Mae's brothers had visited her there a few weeks earlier after getting out of the Navy.

The *Lowell Sun* reported on June 2, 1908, that Thomas O'Reilly, Mae's brother who visited her in New York, told reporters she was married to a man who worked in a New York department store. Mae was, as we know, already married to Julius.

Doyle later changed his story, saying Mae had married a telegraph operator and moved out west, where she died. His wife,

ROCHESTER'S MURDERED MUSIC
TEACHER AND HER ALLEGED SLAYER,

MISS FLORENCE MACFARLANE   MRS. LULU YOUNGS.

Florence McFarland and Lulu Youngs, the jealous wife of Florence's
lover. *Photo courtesy of newspapers.com.*

however, again reiterated that Mae was alive, but she refused to
give out an address.

In June of 1907—the time period when Julius said he'd murdered her in La Porte—Mae, according to family, was back in Rochester. That ran counter to the story told by Daniel F. Welch, another
member of the family. He said Mae had lived and worked in New
York for most of the winter of 1908 but was now visiting friends
in Saratoga. That was somewhat confusing as it meant she wasn't
dead and buried out west as Doyle said or living in New York like
her aunt had stated. She also, according to Welch, had never been
to La Porte and had no contact with Julius after his imprisonment.

The Rochester chief of police also believed Mae had died out
west, but he was getting his information from Doyle. On June 11,
1908, the *La Porte Weekly Herald* received a telegram from the Rochester police reporting that they'd been told Mae had moved from

New York City to stay with her new husband's parents. His last name was either Cowan or Welch.

To make it even more confusing, another of Mae's uncles, John Peel (sometimes spelled Teel) said that Mae left Rochester and moved to Syracuse, where, working in a factory, she met and married a man named Cowan. Peel talked to numerous reporters and told a variety of stories to each. But a common theme was that Cowan was a rather wild and dissolute fellow, and soon after their marriage, he forged his father's name to a check. The father had him arrested but refused to sue or prosecute, and the matter was allowed to drop. Young Cowan never had to work because his father was well off, and so, said Peel, his life was one of dissipation.

The O'Reilly-Cowan marriage quickly hit a rough patch, and the couple separated. Peel told one reporter he'd received a letter from Texas signed by a man named Faugh telling him about Cowan's legal problems. The reporter asked to see the letter, but Peel didn't have it any longer. He did hazard a guess that Faugh might actually be Cowan as he recognized the handwriting.

Peel later told the *La Porte Weekly Herald* the letter was signed by Jonathan G. Thaw, but he knew it was written by Julius as he recognized the handwriting. That he recognized the handwriting in itself is interesting, as Mae and Julius hardly knew each other before marrying, and within two weeks, he had abandoned her. That's not a lot of time to become familiar enough with someone's handwriting to recognize it three years later.

While Faugh provided information on Cowan, the Thaw missive asked for the address of Mae's aunt Mrs. John Doyle and also inquired if Mae was dead or alive and, if alive, where she was living. As for Mae, Peel hadn't seen her for three years—two years before Julius claimed to have taken her to New York.

Peel, unlike Doyle, was willing to share Mae's address—the one her brother Thomas had given other relatives. It was 11½ 56th Street in New York City, but whether it was east or west, he didn't know.

Those following the O'Reilly family's different and often contradictory stories will probably not be surprised to find out that when police visited 11½ East 56th, no one by the name of Mae O'Reilly was living there and never had been. A knock on the door at 11½ West 56th Street yielded the same results—no Mae O'Reilly/Truelson/Cowan had ever resided there. If Thomas had stayed with his sister at either address just two or three weeks previously, she'd left quickly afterward and just as quickly vanished from everyone's memory.

The Rochester police were getting pretty tired of all this obfuscation. The *Evening World* reported:

> Acting police chief Michael J Zimmerman took steps today to compel relatives of the missing Mae O'Reilly, supposed to be the wife of Julius Truelson, to tell where she is. Truelson is the man who confessed to being an accomplice of Mrs. Gunness, the La Porte murderess. When Zimmerman sent a detective to question John Doyle, the girl's uncle, in Heisler and Nippert's saloon today, the proprietors refused to let Doyle stop serving drinks and told the sleuth to go where it is warm. Doyle is the man who boasted to a representative of the *Evening World* that he could produce the girl and show letters received from her within a few days, but that it was no one's business where she is.
>
> Chief Zimmerman placed the matter in the hands of Police Court Prosecutor Hogan and a subpoena in John Doe proceedings will be issued for Doyle and his wife and any others who might know where Truelson's wife may have been recently.

So, where was Mae? There were several possible scenarios.

- She was in Saratoga with friends.
- She was living on 11½ East or West 56th Street in New York City, though neighbors said she wasn't and never had.
- She was in Saratoga with the parents of her husband who had the last name of Cowan or Welch.
- She'd married, moved out west, and died.
- She married a man named Cowan in Syracuse who forged a check, and they split up. He moved to Texas and, in an attempt to find out where she was living, sent a letter using the last name of Faugh to her uncle. Or someone named Faugh was writing letters about Cowan getting in trouble with the law in Texas. Faugh's writing looked just like Cowan's.
- She'd quit her job in Rochester because a fellow worker had murdered another coworker.
- She was living in Syracuse but lied to police about her name.
- She was in hiding because of Julius—though he was in jail in Texas.

- She quit her job and left town because Lulu Youngs killed Florence McFarlane, and she didn't want to get involved in what was an open-and-shut case, though she did give a ninety-minute interview about it to a Rochester reporter.
- Her aunt in Rochester knew where she was in living in New York but didn't have or wouldn't give out the address.

To make it even more confusing, in May of 1908, the police commissioner of Saratoga received a letter from Vernon, Texas (the same city where Julius was incarcerated), signed by "John Taylor," asking for information about Mae O'Reilly. It was supposed that Taylor was Truelson.

What we do know is:

- Julius said he took Mae to Belle's farm, Belle murdered her, and he and Ray, who was working part-time for Belle at the time, buried Mae near the railroad tracks on the farm.
- Some of Mae's jewelry, including a ring inscribed with her name, was found when police began digging up the dead.
- The Rochester police, when first contacted by La Porte, tried to find Mae and discovered she had disappeared about the time Julius said he took her to La Porte.
- None of the authorities or newspaper reporters talked to Mae directly. Any information about Mae came only from family members, and they couldn't get their stories straight. In fact, her uncle John Doyle said she had died out west. La Porte was west of New York, though that wasn't likely what he meant.

It's all very complicated, but for those who believe in conspiracies, consider the following. Julius did kill his wife, and after confessing to doing so, his family went into damage-control mode. They paid off Mae's family and asked them to lie to protect Julius— which could explain why Julius's family ran out of money, as they did.

"My brother is crazy," said Harry Truelson of Julius. "He was struck by a trolley car at Twenty-third Street and Broadway five years ago and has been crazy since then. He was paroled from Elmira Reformatory the 1st of last January, and he was a prisoner when Mrs. Gunness was actively killing persons. He was sent to

A postcard of the farm after the murders. *Photo courtesy of the Steve Shook Collection.*

the reformatory for deserting from the army and navy. His story is ridiculous."

Harry also said his family had exhausted every effort to reform Julius and they would no longer have anything to do with him. The family was so ashamed, they'd left Manhattan and were living in a small house in back of the Raunt—once a Long Island railroad stop on the Rockaway Beach branch. It had no address and no station house as it was just a dropping-off point for fishermen using a small island in Jamaica Bay.

Taking in the social mores of the time, Mae's family had other reasons to lie—shame and fear of disgrace.

Julius said that after he helped bury four people, including Jennie, in a pit at Belle's, he came to the uneasy realization that Belle wasn't just a really incompetent midwife but a murderer and told her so. Luckily, she put up with his accusations, and instead of killing him, she made him an offer.

"She quieted me by saying she would pay me handsomely," he said, according to the *Elmira Star-Gazette* in their June 3, 1908, edition. "After giving me $500 I went back to New York City and in May 1907, I went to Saratoga, N.Y. and got my wife, who was in a house of prostitution, and took her to La Porte, telling her I had made a

The Raunt. *Photo courtesy of Library of Congress.*

home for her. I wanted to be free from her so I could marry again, so I wrote to Mrs. Gunness and told her, and after she told me to bring her there, which I did, on June 2, 1907, and Lamphere and I buried her near the railroad track in the rear of the Gunness farm."

The *Fort Wayne Daily News* reported, "Absinthe, cocaine and women, blamed by Truelson for his downfall, have not leavened his emotions. For a month he has filled his jailor's ears with the weirdest tales of crimes and remorse, related with floods of passion and penitence."

If Julius was into absinthe and cocaine, maybe Mae was an addict as well and turned to prostitution to support her habit. If so, her family may have tried to cover it up by running a Mae shell game (she's here, she's there) and, though they knew she was dead, didn't want to acknowledge it for fear the scandal would tarnish the family name.

Julius's complete confession covered nineteen typewritten pages and went into the most minute details of his career, starting in 1903. After reading through it, Sheriff Albert Smutzer decided to visit Julius in Vernon, Texas, to question him in person.

"It is the most remarkable document," said Sheriff Smutzer as reported by *Salt Lake Tribune* on June 3, 1908, "but we are not willing as yet to make it public because we wish to see how much of the truth he is telling. Truelson told things that could only be told by a person familiar with the murder. He described the Gunness house in detail, and I don't see how he could have done it unless he had been there. Although we have no particular faith in his confession."

Julius had impressed Albert with his intelligence and knowledge when he met with him. Julius was able to correctly answer questions like what Belle's wheelbarrow was made of (wood not metal) that even casual visitors to the farm wouldn't know. Albert told Julius that going back to Indiana most likely meant the gallows. And so, by the time the sheriff left Texas, Julius had recanted his confession, choosing to go to jail for fraud rather than to the gallows.

Was Julius telling the truth about his wife being murdered and buried in the field near the railroad track behind the house? There's no definitive answer, but there's a good possibility he was. The best way to find out would have been to excavate that area. But Albert didn't give the order to have it done. Supposedly, he went out to the farm one day when no one else was there and dug up the site. He reported back that the body wasn't there. Case closed. Julius was lying, he couldn't be believed—and his confession was a fantasy. But the bottom line was that no one ever saw Mae again, and eager reporters and police were constantly looking for her.

When Julius countered by saying that if they brought him to La Porte he'd locate her grave, no one took him up on his offer. It was taken as a given that Mae wasn't buried at Belle's. At least at first.

The *Sun and New York Press* reported on November 12, 1908, "The finding of the bones confirms the story of Julius Truelson, the son of a New York manufacturer who told the story of the Gunness murders while confined in a Texas jail, but whose recital did not at the time impress the authorities. The new graves were found in the exact spot described by Truelson and the rest of his story, which implicated Ray Lamphere in a plot to burn the Gunness home, is now receiving more credence from the authorities."

It's likely that Julius didn't tell his next bride, the beautiful Sarah Arabella Vreeland, about the fate of his first wife when they married on March 2, 1908.

"My daughter was introduced to Truelson several months before the marriage," Cornelius Vreeland told reporters from the *Plymouth*

Inquirer on June 4, 1908. "The two took a liking to one another and Belle got my permission to be married. The ceremony was performed on March 2 last in New Jersey. The two went to Montreal.

"About a week afterward I got a letter from Truelson's father in which he said his son already was married and had the father known of the second affair he would have warned me in time. In the meantime, my daughter arrived in Montreal. About eight days after the wedding her husband told her he must leave for a day or two to attend to business."

When Arabella saw Julius reading a letter from Belle, she asked to see it. When he refused, she accused him of corresponding with another woman and broke down in tears.

Luckily for her, when Julius left Montreal, he left her behind. He gave Arabella a check to pay their bill at the Montreal Chateau Champlain, and it bounced.

"I had to pay $100 to obtain my daughter's release from a cell in Montreal, as a bad check given by Truelson had made trouble," said Vreeland, sounding very peevish. "She came back here to live and has neither seen nor heard from Truelson since."

Vreeland said his daughter knew nothing of Mrs. Gunness. He added that he was making inquiries through his lawyer to learn whether Mae O'Reilly was alive at the time of his daughter's marriage to Truelson. The result of the investigation, according to Vreeland, would determine whether his daughter would bring action for annulment or divorce.

Arabella also had less-than-kind words to say about her husband. Despite her father's words that the unhappy couple had known each other for months, it appeared it was more like days. "Don't you believe what Truelson says about being connected with that bad woman in Indiana," Arabella said. "He never knew her. He just concocted that story because he knows I am suing for annulment and he wanted to make it appear that Miss O'Reilly is dead. He is a coward."

Julius's story was that he wanted to hide out at Belle's with Arabella until his father's anger about marrying again died down. It is not clear how he was going to convince a sophisticated and beautiful New York woman to spend the rest of her honeymoon on a pig farm in Indiana, but it turned out he didn't need to. After writing to Belle to say they were going to visit, he received a reply saying he should come alone as the situation was hot and authorities were making inquiries about why so many people seemed to disappear after visiting Belle.

Julius's confession also mentioned that he helped bury Frank Reidinger, but like Mae, there was some dispute about whether Frank was really dead.

Frank Reidinger, who lived in Wisconsin, took out two mortgages on his property and left town, telling people he was going to La Porte to marry a rich widow. When relatives, trying to locate him, contacted Belle, she told them he'd gone west. It was assumed Frank was another of her victims.

Because of the unpaid mortgages, the Waukesha County Clerk's office auctioned off Frank's farm and equipment for $58,000. After the mortgages were paid off, the remaining money—$561 ($16,000)—belonged to Frank, if he was still alive.

Soon after the auction, a letter arrived from a man identifying himself as Frank Reidinger. He stated he was living in Nebraska and wanted the $561 sent to him.

It was the first anyone had heard from Frank since he left Wisconsin to marry the widow in La Porte, and those who knew him thought there was something sketchy about it all. Why, they wondered, was he finally contacting the clerk's office after all this time? Where had he been? If he truly was alive, then why hadn't he paid off the mortgages instead of waiting until there was only $561 left? And more than that, Frank's friend agreed, the handwriting wasn't like his at all.

Albert also wasn't buying the story.

"I cannot understand," said Sheriff Smutzer, "why Reiding [sic] should write to his hired man and instruct him to sell the Wisconsin farm and deposit the money in the bank. That letter was unsigned, and I believe it was written by someone else."

Indeed, unless the letter was written by someone pretending to be Frank hoping to con the estate out of the remaining money, the whole situation didn't make sense. It would be nice to report there was a follow-up story stating that Frank had appeared in person at the Waukesha County Clerk's office, where everyone knew him and congratulated him on his good luck of escaping the clutches of

Sheriff Albert Smutzer, on the left. *Photo courtesy of the La Porte County Historical Society.*

the murderess, and collected his $561. But there were no follow-up stories about Frank.

Indeed, if Belle had escaped, she might have written the letter, hoping to get the last few dollars out of another of her luckless victims. The brief and mysterious appearance of a letter purportedly from Frank isn't conclusive proof that he survived his time down on the farm. After all, why should Frank have fared any better than other visitors to the farm, such as Ole Budsberg, whose son Mat Budsberg arrived from Iola, Wisconsin, in search of his father.

Mat Budsberg's deposition, which tells the story of his father, was taken on May 7, 1908:

Mat Budsberg being duly sworn deposes as follows:

My name is Mat Budsberg. I came to La Porte, reaching here this afternoon, for the purpose of viewing remains of a body which it was thought might be that of my father. The last time I saw my father alive was April 5, 1907. He was then at his home, and mine, about a mile and a half from Iola, Wisconsin. He was a farmer there, living on his own farm. He was, if living, is, a Norwegian. He spoke broken English. He took a Norwegian newspaper called *Skandianven* and another called *Decorah Posten* published in Decorah, Iowa. He

Searchers stand near a recently unearthed head. *Photo courtesy of the Steve Shook Collection.*

left home April 5, 1907, to come to La Porte and run a farm for Mrs. Gunness. . . . Before coming home he had told his brother that he was going away to be married. When he left home, he had with him, according to what the cashier of the bank said, about eight hundred dollars in cash and a draft for one thousand dollars.

Mat produced a letter from a cashier in Iola telling of the burning of Mrs. Gunness's residence and stating that Mrs. Gunness had said Ole stayed in La Porte about a week. But his father, Mat said, was planning on staying in La Porte permanently and even bought some seed potatoes and had them sent from Iola to the farm.

His father had promised to write when he reached the Gunness residence, but the family never heard from him and began to worry. Mat and his brothers wrote to their father.

We wrote two letters and sent some insurance papers for him to sign. It was about a week after he left that I wrote—about two to three weeks after he left that my brother Lewis wrote. My letter was returned to me from the dead letter office in Washington.

Before my letter had come back to me through the dead letter office, a letter came from Mrs. Gunness, addressed to my father. We opened it. In it she said she wanted to send him some letters and papers that had come for him after he left her house, so she wanted to know whether he was at his home to receive them if she sent them there. She said, too, that she hoped he was not offended by her not marrying him.

She said she never thought he would ask her because she had not encouraged him any. She said she hoped, if he was going out west, he would find some land as a homestead; but if she were in his place, she would go to the old country and visit. That's about all. The letter was written in the Norwegian language. Then we thought he had gone out west, and we did not look for him anymore.

April 5, 1907, he had borrowed a hundred dollars at the Farmers' State Bank in Iola, for six months. When the note was due the bank tried to hunt him up. The bank went down here to this Mrs. Gunness and she wrote back that he had been robbed in Chicago of most of his money and some clothes and that he had told her he would go west and try to make up what he had been robbed of before any of his relatives should have learned about it. She said he had left at her house his trunk and a few clothes and would send for them as soon as he got settled down. We still had no suspicion of his having been harmed by Mrs. Gunness. We had no such suspicion until we read in the paper of the burning of Mrs. Gunness's house and that it had always been a mysterious house. Then I told Mr. Edwin Chapin of Iola that I was coming down here, and I asked him to come along. Later we received telegrams from the La Porte Savings Bank and from Sheriff Smutzer and we came down, arriving here this afternoon.

This afternoon I viewed, in the carriage house on the Gunness place, the remains of an unidentified man. I think they were the remains of my father, but I would not swear to it. The size and shape of the head are the same as size and shape of my father's head. The mustache is like my father's which curled down over the mouth. Teeth are, I should think, like my father's, but I am not sure. These are the only points upon which I base the statement that I think the body is that of my father, Ole O. Budsberg.

13

The Theory of the Exploding Head

AS TIME WENT ON AND SEARCHERS FOUND NO TRACE OF THE missing head, more people began to doubt Belle had perished in the fire and now thought the decapitated corpse was a red herring—a way to hide that fact. Coroner Mack, describing himself as harried with doubt, hesitated to declare Belle dead without further proof, emphasizing he had never permitted the official record to describe the woman's corpse as being Mrs. Gunness.

"I shall have to have more evidence before I am satisfied that it is her," Mack was quoted as saying in an article in the *Chicago Tribune* on May 8, 1908. He questioned not only why a head hadn't been discovered but also why there were no teeth in the smoldering remains.

The pressure was on Sheriff Smutzer, who wanted to end any speculation that Belle was still alive, so he took the step of hiring Louis "Klondike" Schultz, a former miner who had panned for gold in the Klondike, a region in the Yukon that was the epicenter of the Gold Rush of 1897–1899. But Klondike wasn't looking for a head—though finding that would have been nice as well. He was looking for Belle's bridgework.

Working under a somewhat ludicrous hypothesis that the missing skull might have exploded in the fire, which is why searchers couldn't find it, Albert was given the job of locating the dental work performed the year before. Belle had paid Dr. I. P. Norton $40 for a

The sluicing system set up by Klondike. *Photo courtesy of the Steve Shook Collection.*

plate of false teeth for her upper jaw, 22 karat gold crowns on her lower bicuspids, and a bridge consisting of four porcelain teeth, each backed by more 22 karat gold.

Since a house fire burns at around 1,100 degrees Fahrenheit and gold can withstand temperatures up to about 1,800 degrees, theoretically her teeth should have still been lying undisturbed in the ruins of the house.

When Wirt learned Albert hired Klondike to search for the dental work, he was angry; he became more incensed upon learning Albert had Dr. Norton draw a diagram of the teeth to give to Klondike.

"Evidence is now being deliberately manufactured to make it fit the theory of the detectives," he said at the time, adding that there was no doubt that a set of gold teeth similar to Belle's and bearing the dentist's special identification marks would be found.

Wirt's words didn't stop Klondike from proceeding. With an avid crowd of onlookers, he built a sluice on the cellar floor and began to sift through the debris. It was slow going, and over a week passed before Klondike finally struck gold, or gold and porcelain. After leaning over to pluck something out of the sluice, he held up what appeared to be Belle's bridge. It was proof, Albert said, that Belle was dead. In jubilation, he threw his leather cap in the air.

Not so fast, said Joe Maxson, who, along with his brother-in-law Isaiah "Peck" Aldrafer, had been working around the yard the morning the teeth were found. Joe said he saw Klondike pull the bridgework from his pocket, saying he found what he had been looking for. Peck corroborated Joe's testimony, testifying he'd seen Klondike remove them from his right pocket.

Joe and Peck weren't the only ones suspicious about the find.

"I looked carefully under the woman's body to find some trace of a missing head," said La Porte Police Chief Clinton Cochrane, who had been among the first to search the cellar after the fire. "There was nothing there to suggest a skull. There was not a sign of gold or porcelain or any other kind of teeth." Cochrane was convinced Belle left the body of a headless woman in the burning house and made her escape.

But despite this testimony, Dr. Norton identified the dental work as his, adding in his opinion they could not have been removed from Mrs. Gunness's mouth while she was alive without splitting the gold crowns. Coroner Mack, then, finally declared Belle dead.

There was no apparent reason for Klondike to fake finding the teeth unless it was at the behest of the man who hired him—Albert Smutzer. Wirt was among those who believed the sheriff wanted to prove Belle was dead, see Ray convicted of murder, and prevent any further investigation that might lead to his involvement.

Out of the forty witnesses called to appear in front of the grand jury, Klondike was the only one who disregarded the summons, nor did he show up to testify at the trial. No one knew where he was, though some said he'd gone out west and others mentioned Little Rock as his next destination.

Whoever was paying for Ray's defense (many thought it was Liz Smith) certainly got their money's worth. Wirt, along with attorneys Ellsworth Weir and Lemuel Darrow, went into overdrive to prove that the bridgework had been manufactured and planted at the scene. Hiring two local doctors, Wirt tasked them with fashioning a facsimile of Belle's dental work. Then, they placed the bridgework in a blacksmith's forge, trying to recreate the conditions of the house fire. The heat caused several teeth to crumble, pitted the porcelain of others, and somewhat melted the gold.

Wirt called O. P. M. Squires, a La Porte jeweler, to the stand. Squires testified the gold had been melted right off several watches found in the debris. It seemed odd then that the gold caps on Belle's teeth had somehow survived the blaze without even being fused together.

Wirt also asked the jeweler to compare the gold in the bridgework Klondike had found to the gold in the watches and jewelry retrieved from the cellar. The latter showed the effects of the fire. Klondike's gold didn't.

Calling W. H. Ludwig, who had previously worked in a Los Angeles crematorium, to the witness stand, Wirt asked him to explain that temperatures of 2,600 degrees or higher are needed to turn a body into cremains. A house fire wouldn't do it. Even more telling, flesh and bones burn to ash before the skull does, said Ludwig. It was always the last to go.

These testimonies were a huge boost to Ray's defense. Judge Richter, the presiding judge who at first had admitted the coroner's verdict, reversed himself. Belle Gunness was no longer considered dead.

But as dramatic as Wirt could be, it was his partner Weir, the son of a former senator, who stole the scene; he requested that Belle Gunness be summoned to appear in court. When asked why, he replied it was his opinion that Belle wasn't so far away she couldn't respond to the subpoena.

Wirt, Weir, and Darrow kept scoring points.

Two boys who were playing near Pine Lake Cemetery testified they saw Belle after the fire. She had raised her veil to take a sip from the water pump and then, after seeing the boys staring at her, hurried along with her male companion back into the buggy.

When did it happen? Wirt asked them.

"The Thursday after Independence Day" was the reply. Wirt glanced at his pocket calendar and then read the date aloud: "July 9."

Wirt also introduced evidence showing Belle was seen on the Saturday before the fire riding in a buggy with a woman of small stature. The same woman was later spotted walking on Belle's property. And then, like so many others, she was never seen again. It wasn't Belle in the fire, according to Wirt; the body was too small. It was this other stranger, the one who was there one day and gone the next.

Prosecutor Ralph Smith countered. Burned meat drastically shrinks in size, he said, an apt if not very appealing comparison.

Sorting through the boxes of severed legs, arms, feet, heads, and other human remains, the doctors conducting the autopsies noted how expertly the victims had been butchered into pieces. *Photo courtesy of the La Porte County Historical Society.*

Wirt also attempted to show that the sheriff knew about and even aided in covering up Belle's crimes. It was a common sentiment among La Porte residents, who often noticed Albert's red runabout parked in front of Belle's house. The car was also tied to the crime in other ways.

Louise Gackle, who worked at a La Porte shirt factory, testified that at 3 a.m. on the morning of April 28, the date of the Gunness fire, a red automobile, covered with canvas, passed her window. Gackle lived on Park Avenue, the road running directly from La Porte to the Gunness farm. Others spotted the red roadster as well that night as it sped through Hobart and Valparaiso, two towns west of La Porte and not far from Chicago.

Albert Smutzer, Wirt said, had such a car. Indeed he did. But so did someone else.

The *Cincinnati Enquirer* reported:

In the cross-examination of Sheriff Smutzer, Attorney Worden for the defense, by his questions, tried to throw suspicion upon the officer by intimating that Sheriff Smutzer had been at the Gunness place in his automobile. This Smutzer denied.

On redirect examination Prosecutor Smith asked Smutzer if there was in town any other automobile like his. To this the Sheriff replied:

"Yes, Attorney Worden has one."

No one seriously considered Wirt to be the one driving the car that was often parked in front of Belle's house or that roared through town in the early morning hours as fire consumed the house. All eyes remained fixed on Albert.

According to Ray, Belle got away with the macabre operation as long as she did because a highly placed local official was taking hush money from her. On one occasion, Ray said, he walked into the house just as the unnamed official was pocketing a wad of bills. After the man had gone, Belle said, "I not only had to buy him an automobile, but I just gave him another thousand dollars."

"Sheriff Smutzer was suspected [because] some believed he helped her get away," said Dorothy Rowley, who worked at the La Porte County Historical Society Museum for nearly twenty years serving as an associate curator and was also appointed by the governor of Indiana as the first La Porte County historian, a position she held for ten years. "His car, a little red runabout, had been seen out there at the Gunness place quite a bit. People remembered seeing the car because of its bright color."

Rowley, considered the resident expert on Belle Gunness when she was working at the historical society, believed Belle had escaped the fire. So did others.

"The sheriff's runabout was the talk of the town," said Bruce Johnson, the producer of a movie on the Gunness case and board member of the La Porte Historical Society. "They'd ask how he could afford it and talked about him being in partnership with Belle."

Fern Eddy Schultz, La Porte County historian, noted there have long been rumors that the sheriff was having an affair with the widow, though, she cautions, there was no proof.

More than once Albert was quoted as saying he believed Belle had an accomplice, one who was much brighter than Ray. Was he referring to himself?

At some point, Albert must have become aware of the rumors about his connection with Belle. Maybe he was trying to bring an end to speculation about their relationship when he told news

The jury at Ray Lamphere's trial for the murder of Belle Gunness.
Photo courtesy of the La Porte County Historical Society.

reporters that he had confronted Belle, accusing her of murdering the many men who came to stay with her. She denied doing so, he said. After that, when Belle saw Albert, or so he said, she invited him to come visit. He was suspicious and declined her invitations.

In the end, despite his defense team's best efforts, Ray didn't walk out of the courtroom a free man. Ten of the men on the jury believed the handyman was guilty of both murder and arson. But ultimately two holdouts, four ballots, and over twenty-four hours of deliberation brought about a convoluted verdict. Judge Richter had instructed the jury they could find for arson only, and that's what they did. Belle Gunness was dead and Ray had set the house on fire, the jury foreman announced, but he wasn't guilty of murder. He was sentenced to two to twenty-one years in prison.

He was also fined $5,000 (or about $140,000 today) for the destruction of Belle's property, disenfranchised for five years, and, if he failed to pay his fine, could spend more time in the local jail after being released from prison until he was able to do so.

It was a lucky break for Ray, who appeared very relieved. Wirt, on the other hand, was outraged. He would appeal the case and take it to the supreme court if necessary, he vowed. But as the *La Porte*

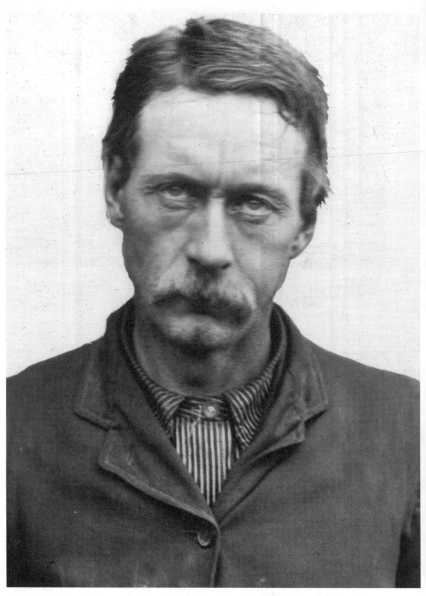

Ray Lamphere. *Photo courtesy of the La Porte County Historical Society.*

Weekly Herald reported on December 3, 1908, the transcript alone, which was necessary for an appeal, could cost as much as $500. Ray's family had no money, and whoever had been paying Wirt up to this point might not have been able or willing to do so any longer.

Besides, an appeal would not reach the supreme court in less than two years. By that time, the minimum term of the sentence, two years, would have expired, and it would be better to work for his release on parole.

Many newspaper editors had a problem with the verdict. The *Chicago News* stated that if Belle had been on trial, perhaps Ray's jury would have fined her for not having secured a license to conduct a graveyard. The *Lafayette Journal* pointed out that if Belle and her children perished in the fire and Ray set fire to the house, he is guilty of their murder. But the jury did not reason in this manner. According to the verdict, we may conclude that Mrs. Gunness is alive, if she wasn't murdered, and that she should have been killed anyway.

Albert accompanied Ray to the state prison in Michigan City, and on the journey, Ray told the sheriff, who had tried so hard to get him convicted of murder, that he was lucky he might be spending the next two decades locked up. "Why, I might have been chopped up and put in a hole in Old Woman Gunness's chicken yard," Ray said, exalted in his lucky break.

It would all turn out to be a moot point. Ray didn't even reach the two-year mark. By the end of the next year he would be dead from tuberculosis.

14

The Missing

NEWS OF THE GUNNESS MURDER FARM SPREAD ACROSS THE nation, and many came to believe that their missing loved ones were buried there. Some wrote letters of inquiry, and others made the sad pilgrimage there, hoping to find their loved one and bring about some type of peace through closure. However, Belle's heavy hand with quicklime and her signature method of dismembering bodies and burying them in gunnysacks made identification difficult, if not impossible, particularly for anyone who had been buried a year or more. In some cases, jewelry or other belongings found on the farm provided all the evidence some families needed.

Jens G. Render was looking for his half-brother, John O. Moe, whom he had not seen since January 2, 1906. In May 1908, he learned that Moe had made withdrawals at the First National Bank in La Porte. Render took the train to La Porte and immediately went to the First National Bank. He showed a photo of his half-brother to Alfred Peglow, an assistant cashier. Peglow recognized John Moe as a man who had come in with Belle Gunness to withdraw money from his account.

Peglow, eager to help, suggested Render visit How's Jewelry Store to look for his half-brother's watch. Render was able to identify Moe's watch by its manufacturing number. Albert and Prosecuting Attorney Smith were informed, and they took Render to view the bodies. Given their state of putrefaction, Render was unable to determine if any of the body parts belonged to Moe.

"But I feel entirely content that he lost his life at the Gunness place in Center Township, La Porte County," he said.

Tonnes Peterson Lien of Rushford, Minnesota, answered a newspaper advertisement placed by a wealthy widow. Shortly after, Tonnes sewed his money into his sleeve and set off to La Porte, Indiana, to be married. His brother, Samuel Peterson Lien, became worried after not having heard from his brother in quite some time. He first visited Rushford and there found that no one had seen or heard from Tonnes since he left for La Porte.

Samuel read about the murder farm and, with a sinking feeling, next headed to Indiana. He met with Wirt Worden and told him about his missing brother. Wirt asked Samuel if he would be able to recognize his brother's body. He was sure he could and added that another identifying feature was the heavy silver watch Tonnes always carried, which had his initials scratched on the case.

Wirt remembered seeing such a watch, but when they looked at the victims' watches being held at the prosecutor's office, it wasn't among them. Fortunately, the jewelers who examined the watches found on the farm had kept a list, and a description of Tonnes's watch was among them. It appeared that Tonnes indeed had come to La Porte but had not left.

In 1907, forty-three-year-old Abraham Phillips, a wealthy landowner, left Bellington, West Virginia, to marry a rich widow with a large farm in Northern Indiana. He did not sell his farm or personal property before leaving but took with him a large sum of money. He never returned. Phillips was a member of the Brotherhood of Railway Trainmen, and a watch that had been engraved with a locomotive was found during the search of the Gunness house's remains. The *Daily Review* reported, "Phillips' relatives will be advised of this strange circumstance and his name may be added to the known victims of the murderess."

Others made inquiries of La Porte because the town was a piece of the puzzle in the missing person's story.

George Berry, from Tuscola, Illinois, told his employer that he was going to La Porte to marry Mrs. Gunness. He sold his small farm and took $1,500 with him. He was never seen again.

A tombstone dedicated to all the unidentified victims. *Photo courtesy of Dale Hoppe.*

Olaf Jensen left Chicago in 1906 to visit a wealthy widow in La Porte. He took with him only a small handbag and a large sum of money that he planned to "invest in the widow's farm." When his family did not hear from him, they advertised for him in the *Skandinaven*. They received a letter stating he was in Boston, but they were unable to locate him there.

Sheriff Smutzer received a letter from the acting consul for Norway in Chicago and a letter from Jensen's mother inquiring about the missing man. According to the *St. Joseph Daily Press*, Jensen was known to have been at the Gunness farm, where he assisted in the moving of a vault.

"His disappearance was explained by Mrs. Gunness with her usual versatility," wrote the reporter. "Jensen has gone out west," she said. "He didn't like La Porte."

Coroner Mack also received inquiries about missing persons, such as one from Osage County, Kansas, which concerned Emil Tell, who left with $3,000 to go to La Porte and hadn't been heard from since.

Christen Hilkven mysteriously disappeared from Dover, Wisconsin, in 1906 after selling his farm for $2,000 in cash. His friends believed he was a victim of Belle Gunness because he had had his address changed to La Porte and the postmaster at La Porte said his mail was delivered at the Gunness farm.

E. J. Tiefland, from Minneapolis, went to La Porte after corresponding with Belle, who had advertised in a Minneapolis newspaper. He was not seen after.

Abe Mills from Knox County, Missouri, was lured to St. Joseph, Michigan, by a matrimonial advertisement. He then left his wife and family for La Porte, Indiana. Officers believed he became a victim of Gunness.

Mrs. Benjamin F. Carling of Chicago inquired in person in La Porte. She viewed the bodies and was able to identify one of them as likely belonging to her husband. She noted the contour of the head, the hair color, and the fact that certain teeth were missing. Carling was an insurance man who was "believed to have fallen into Mrs. Gunness's clutches through a proposed land deal."

Ann Tillman of Kenosha, Wisconsin, disappeared two years before the fire at the Gunness farm. Her last letter stated that she was ill and had been invited to the country to rest. Many citizens of Kenosha believed that Tillman was one of Belle's victims. In a *Chicago Tribune* article, she was identified as Mrs. Anna Tilleman Groeger of Kenosha who vanished after writing relatives to say she was going to rest on a farm near La Porte.

Some people were unable to make a direct connection to La Porte or Belle, but inquired about their missing loved ones nonetheless.

Herman Konitzer went missing from Chicago in January of 1906 after having been in the country for only three months. His friends believed he was among Belle's victims and that he was in fact the "man from Chicago" that Ray described. Belle had said this man went south for his health.

James Kane of Tunnel, New York, left his home with the intention of going west and marrying a widow. His relatives traced him to Chicago but no further. They believed he was one of Belle's victims.

Mrs. John Horatio McJunkin inquired with the sheriff about her husband, who had been missing for three years. She was convinced that he was among those buried on the Gunness farm, and her description did in fact match that of one of the bodies.

On November 28, 1902, Clara Witzler walked out of the family home in Perrysburg, Ohio, and was never seen again. Clara wasn't a typical runaway—she was educated in a time when few girls earned a college degree, and her family was well-to-do and socially prominent.

The daughter of William and Hannah Witzler, Clara (sometimes called Frances in news reports) was born in 1875. In 1895, she graduated from Valparaiso University, one of the nation's first coeducational colleges, with a bachelor of science degree. The university, located in Valparaiso, Indiana, was just twenty-five miles west of La Porte.

When the fire consumed the house on the Gunness farm, Clara had been missing for almost six years. Her mother, hearing about the fire and the bodies buried at the farm, wondered if Clara could be one of them.

The *Detroit Free Press* reported:

Mrs. Henry Witzler of Toledo walked among the dead at the morgue this morning, hoping that there might be some mark of identification on one of the skeleton forms which would prove that her daughter was one of the victims of the house of tragedy.

Tears coursed down the mother's cheeks as she looked upon the headless and dismembered bodies. There was no identification but the Toledo woman, hoping that some tragedy might solve the mystery of her daughter's strange disappearance, came to La Porte. Like scores of others she came in the hope that the Gunness murders would bring closure to the mystery which she had vainly

The remains of Andrew Helgelien. *Photo courtesy of the La Porte County Historical Society.*

labored to solve since 1902, when Frances Witzler, young and pretty, a college graduate, with life before her, left her home never to return.

Esther Worchowski was just sixteen when she answered an advertisement for work in Indiana and left Chicago. She was last seen in Northern Indiana by a family friend, but the friend could not remember the name of the town. Worchowski's brother Max contacted authorities when he read about the corpses discovered at the Gunness farm, saying he thought one of the female bodies might be his sister. Unfortunately so few of the bodies, due to quicklime and butchery, were identifiable.

Occasionally there would be a letter among the inquiries from someone who had survived Belle. Sheriff Smutzer received a letter from I. N. Youtsler of Caspar, Wyoming, describing a night of terror he spent on the Gunness farm a year before the fire. A peddler, he had stopped by the house with $700 in his pocket and been invited in. When Belle learned he was partially deaf, she began openly plotting his murder. Youtsler armed himself and walked the floor of his room ready for an attack all night. He fled at first light.

Neighbors came forward with their own stories and inquiries as well.

Edward Canary, a young man of limited intelligence who had gotten on Belle's nerves and lived just a mile from her farm, disappeared in 1906. His mother was certain Belle had something to do with his disappearance.

Mrs. William Deisslen, who lived just a short distance from the Gunness farm, told the police about the disappearance of a baby, a girl, and a man. Mrs. Deisslen often visited Belle. One time, she said, she heard a baby crying upstairs. She went to investigate and found an infant lying on a bed sobbing. Mrs. Deisslen comforted the baby, and it fell asleep. When she visited next, the baby was gone. Neither Mrs. Deisslen nor Belle mentioned it, and the matter soon dropped.

The second victim, according to Mrs. Deisslen, was a beautiful girl from Chicago. Belle met her at the train station and took her back to the farm. She was seen on the farm for a little while but then disappeared.

The third disappearance was that of a man. Mrs. Deisslen said a peddler stopped at the Gunness farm, hitched his horse to the gate post, and went inside. But he never came out. The horse remained hitched for hours. Later, Belle was seen with it about the farm.

In addition to the inquiries made of these—and many more—missing persons, there were also those who believed that several of serial killer Johann Hoch's victims were buried on the Gunness farm. Hoch's murderous sojourn through Northern Indiana convinced many, including grieving relatives and police, that he and

Visitors stand outside the make-shift morgue on Belle's property.
Photo courtesy of the Steve Shook Collection.

Belle were partners in crime. He seduced women into marriage, took their cash, ended their lives, and shipped them to Belle's farm.

Whether Hoch and Gunness were business partners is a tantalizing question. There's a list of women who married Hoch and disappeared. Because he lived in cities, he didn't have the disposal opportunities that Belle did. There was also testimony that indicated Belle had a German accomplice.

After the fire, officials in La Porte received lots of mail, most of which could be filed under weird and anonymous, but every so often one showed promise, including a letter sent to La Porte Chief of Police Clinton Cochrane by Fred Hafle, a retired mechanic who lived in a Cleveland suburb. The letter claimed that Belle had an accomplice in her matrimonial schemes and was accompanied by a photo of a woman who looked like a younger version of Belle.

> Dear Sir:
>
> Last August while waiting for a streetcar in our public square I was approached by a man who began a conversation with me. He stated he was in Cleveland on a speculation and the cattle was his line. After some time, he endeavored to find out regarding my family, etc., and asked me if I was married. In a spirit of fun, I said

no, and he immediately began to tell me about a rich widow who resided in La Porte, Ind., who was looking for a man.

He claimed she was the owner of a large ranch, stocked with cattle, and that she was looking for a man. When I asked him why she could not get a man there, he replied that she did not want a man from that part of the country and he also stated that if I was willing both he and I would get on the train and go there at once.

When I said I did not like to do that, he said if I would pay the fare the woman should come at once and I could see for myself.

The man claimed that Chicago was his home. He was about 35 or 36 years of age, five feet, three or four inches tall and weighed about 160 pounds. He had a reddish complexion, smooth face, dark hair, and wore a soft black hat, blue suit, and had the general appearance of a man pretty well to do.

Hafle said that the man was German and they spoke in German. "The man did not give me his name," Hafle said, "nor the name of the woman. I had forgotten the name of the town in Indiana until reminded by the dispatches from La Porte telling of the Gunness woman. The stranger took my name and address and said he would write. After talking with him a while we went to a hotel where he was stopping. There he got his suitcase and coat and left after asking me to meet him at the hotel the next morning. I never saw him afterward."

The photo of the woman the man gave to Hafle was later placed under a powerful microscope. The rings on the woman's fingers in that photograph were identified as those taken from the fingers of the headless body found in the ruins of the Gunness farmhouse.

Belle was long suspected of doing business with matrimonial agencies, such as the Blackney agency, in different areas and even owning a few in nearby small towns like Syracuse and Warsaw where she operated an agency under the name of Beller Hinckley. She also frequented the Spotlight Agency in St. Joseph, Michigan, and one lucky man said he'd been promised a match with a rich farm woman in La Porte by the agency. Fortunately he hadn't responded to that ad. Hoch was suspected of murdering several women from Northwest Indiana whose bodies were never found. If it was indeed Hoch who was marrying and murdering women from these small Indiana towns, he may have also combined this with collecting Belle's mail or even used her agencies for letters of his own.

The theory that Hoch and Belle were accomplices (or that she had an accomplice) was bolstered by the testimony of Axel Carlson, a conductor on the interurban electric railroad that ran between La Porte and Michigan City, passing within a half mile of the Gunness home. The nearest station on the line to the Gunness place was number seven at Card's Landing on Pine Lake.

The *St. Louis Post-Dispatch* quoted Conductor Carlson in their September 20, 1908, edition:

> For a year or more, I have noticed a man riding on my car who invariably got off at station No. 7. He always rode out either from La Porte or Michigan City at night. Usually reached station No. 7 about 9 or 10 o'clock. He always carried a grip. After leaving the car, he would hurry into a woodland nearby, where, time after time, I saw him meet a woman in a buggy waiting for him in the shadows.
>
> To her he would give the grip and she would drive off with it toward the Gunness farm. I am convinced now the woman who kept these constant and mysterious trysts was Mrs. Gunness and that the bag which the man carried was filled with answers to her matrimonial advertisements.
>
> Often, too, the man boarded my car at station No. 7. His actions aroused my curiosity and I discussed him with other conductors of the road. By comparing notes we learned that after leaving one car and meeting the woman he never failed to take the next car either to Michigan City or La Porte.

Carlson's description of the man was very similar to the one provided by Fred Hafle of the man he met in Cleveland.

If this mysterious man was Hoch, then it might have been when he was checking mailboxes at Belle's matrimonial agencies that the fate of Mary Schultz was sealed.

In 1900, Albert Buschberg, a wealthy drugstore owner, met and wooed Mary Schultz, a twenty-nine-year-old widow living in the small farming community of Argos, Indiana, about forty-five minutes from La Porte. When she met Buschberg, he must have seemed like a dream come true—a kind, charming man who would take care of her and Nettie, her five-year-old daughter, in a way her deceased husband with his fondness for drink hadn't.

After Mary and Buschberg married, they moved to Chicago. And then no one ever heard from mother and daughter again. Also gone was the money Mary had inherited upon her husband's death. After her disappearance, the sketch of Mary appearing in multiple newspapers throughout the country showed the face of a woman worn thin from a harsh life. Her large eyes stared out with a sadness about life and what it had done to her. She was dressed plainly, and her hair was tightly coiled.

Buschberg was one of the aliases used by Hoch, and claiming to own a drugstore was one of the ruses he used to impress women. Like many of Hoch's wives, Mary was of German descent.

The vanishing of a nondescript woman mired in poverty with few friends or acquaintances who was new to town might have quickly been overlooked. But Mary had a brother, and he wanted to find his sister and his niece.

"Shortly after they arrived in Chicago letters ceased coming to me," her brother, John Frick, an employee of the Nickel Plate Railroad, told police, "and I am under the belief that my sister and her little girl were done away with. My sister had about $1,500 at the time of the marriage."

In May of 1908, when Frick, who was still looking for his sister and niece, learned of the decayed unidentified body of an adult woman and a young girl discovered at the Gunness farm, he hoped to identify them as Mary and Nettie. After all, it was extremely unlikely that Mary and Nettie were still alive, and if they were dead, Belle's was a likely place for them to be.

Mary and Nettie weren't the only victims of Hoch thought to be on the Gunness farm. In his book, *Twenty Years a Detective in the Wickedest City in the World*, the famed Chicago police detective Clifton Rodman Wooldridge writes that Justina Loeffler, a pretty German immigrant who married a man in Chicago and vanished, was "believed to have been married to Johann Hoch and sent by him to Mrs. Gunness to be murdered and buried."

Justina Loeffler, called Tina by her friends, had moved to Elkhart, Indiana, from Baden, Germany, with her maternal uncle when she was fifteen, leaving the home of her mother and three siblings.

While living in Elkhart, Tina conscientiously saved the money she earned working as a domestic. Then, in 1901, deciding she could earn more money in Chicago, she took a job at a restaurant on Wells Street.

Keeping her uncle Jacob Hoeckele and his family in Elkhart apprised of her movements, Tina left the restaurant and next took a position at a private residence "on the boulevard," a phrase indicative of an upscale neighborhood. Shortly after, she sent a letter to the Hoeckeles announcing her upcoming marriage.

On May 22, 1902, a day after the wedding, she visited Elkhart as Mrs. Robert Schmidt. Her husband, she told the Hoeckeles, was a fine-looking man, energetic, thrifty, and ambitious with plans to buy a drugstore. Tina said he couldn't come to Elkhart with her that day because he was too busy at work and wasn't feeling well.

She was excited because she and her new husband were planning a bridal trip to Germany, and in preparation for their trip, the Hoeckeles lent her a trunk and gave her gifts to give her family in Baden.

A few days later, Tina returned to Elkhart. During the few days she was there, her family noticed she seemed changed, no longer fun loving and outgoing the way she'd been before her marriage. Instead, she was despondent. But since Tina wasn't one to talk about her problems, the family learned little about what was going on. They did suppose, when talking among themselves, that she had marital troubles.

A few days after she went back to Chicago, the Hoeckeles received a letter from Tina. She wrote that unfortunately they'd canceled the wedding trip to Germany because her husband was too sick to go. In June, another letter arrived, this time saying all her jewels and valuables had been stolen.

Jacob, concluding that the marriage was "an unfortunate one or at least peculiar," answered her letter with a warning lest "the husband be stolen too," which was his way of telling Tina to keep an eye on the man she'd married.

There were no further letters. Tina was missing. Alarmed, Jacob started investigating, and what he discovered didn't bode well. When Justina left Elkhart to move to Chicago, she had $200 in the St. Joseph Valley Bank of Elkhart, $300 in a Boston bank, and $1,000 in a bank in Germany. The sums represented an inheritance as well as what Tina had saved since moving to America. Contacting the police, Jacob reported all he and his family knew about Tina's husband, recalling an odd statement she'd made about her

The Ruins of the Home of Mrs. Gunness, Near Laporte, Ind. No. 1125

Postcard showing all that remained of the once solid brick home—just bricks and rubble. *Photo courtesy of the Steve Shook Collection.*

husband having a best friend and constant companion who was like a brother to him. The two looked so much alike they could have been twins, Tina had said.

Reverend J. H. Heinz of Elkhart traveled to Chicago, where he and Jacob's brother-in-law who lived in the city began their search for Tina by calling at the Schmidts' last known address.

Too late, they were told. The Schmidts and the man who lived with them had moved away. They hadn't left any information about where they were going, but they all appeared respectable. That was less than assuring, particularly after the family learned Hoch was a close friend of Louis Toombs who was convicted of strangling twenty-three-year-old Carrie Larsen after she had spurned his advances and then dumped her body in the Chicago River.

Toombs was hanged for his crime on August 8, 1902. The family presumed that Toombs was the same man Tina had described as like a brother to her husband and who had lived with them. A very bad sign indeed. More bad news followed when they learned that at the time Tina moved to Chicago, Hoch was going by aliases Robert or George Schmitt or Schmidt and telling people he was the son of wealthy parents in Hamburg, Germany.

Tina was never seen or heard from again.

15

Dead or Alive?

LOUIS BLAKE WAS WORKING AS AN AMBULANCE DRIVER WHEN he received a call to pick up an injured woman at the South Bend train station. He rushed her to Epworth Hospital, now South Bend Memorial Hospital, where his fiancée, Lydia Decker, worked as a student nurse. Lydia had grown up on a farm near the Gunness property, and though the name of the new patient was unfamiliar, she recognized Belle's voice when the patient asked her, "Is your pappy still on the farm?"

Before long, the police entered the hospital in search of Belle. But they were too late. Belle had outsmarted them and escaped. "She had bribed this man . . . and he had gotten a taxi for her and spirited her out of the hospital unknowing to the authorities," said Louis. "She was gone."

If this woman was Belle using a false name, why would she risk blowing her disguise by asking Lydia about her pappy? But then again, it was Belle's nature to skate close to the edge. At least, that was the image of Belle being built at the time.

According to Janet Langlois in *Women's Folklore, Women's Culture*, stories such as Louis's transformed people's perceptions of Belle from a monster who murdered innocents to "a clever woman who inverts the proper role of the sick person in order to outwit representatives of the institutionalized order." Langlois notes that Louis's comments about Belle "being in cahoots" with La Porte

The basement where the bodies of a headless women and three children were found. *Photo courtesy of the La Porte County Historical Society.*

County Sheriff Albert Smutzer—still a virulent rumor while she was conducting research in 1975—dramatized the public's waning belief in the credibility of the executive branch as the underlying chaos revealed itself.

Langlois goes on to say that once Belle began being described as "that tricky Norwegian," a woman who was "too smart" to die in the fire, someone who was able to pull "the wool over everybody's eyes," she became a folk villainess, an outlaw deserving respect for her ability to outwit inept authorities. This portrait of Belle did not fit the theory that she, knowing her crimes were soon to be uncovered, murdered her children and then, after ingesting poison, set herself and her house on fire.

"I cannot believe that she committed suicide or that any farm-hand outwitted and murdered her," said Assistant Chief Schuetter. "I think she is a member of a gang of murderers, organized for the purpose of collecting insurance on their victims." George Anderson, one of the few men who came to the farm and left of their own volition, and May Olander, Jennie Olsen's sister, were also convinced Belle had set fire to her home and was still alive.

It is hard to imagine that an accomplished mass murderer like Belle, who evaded discovery for years, would willingly harm herself.

Arrows on this postcard point to holes in the ground where cadavers or cadaver parts were located. *Photo courtesy of the Steve Shook Collection.*

What is not hard to imagine is that Belle faked her own death and went on the run. This begs the million-dollar question, Where was Belle Gunness?

In June 1908, the *New York Times* reported, "The Detroit police believe they are on the trail of Mrs. Belle Gunness. . . . Two young women . . . are said to have met Mrs. Gunness since her supposed burned body was found in the ruins of her home. The police assert that the statements of the two young women convinced them that Mrs. Gunness is still alive. They gave the names of other persons who are also said to know that the woman is alive, and the police are looking for them."

Another sighting was reported one month later: "An American woman about 50 years old, five feet seven inches in height, dark blue eyes, light chestnut hair, slightly gray, quick nervous step, passed by Palenque. Was traveling alone and without baggage and has no letters of recommendations. Left Salt de Aqua wearing masculine clothing of khaki. Made inquiries of communication with Usumacinta River and plunged into the interior alone, not heeding warnings as to danger." Neither sighting led authorities to anything concrete.

A more substantial sighting came to light in November 1908, during Ray Lamphere's trial, from a man who claimed to have known Belle. Daniel M. Hutson and his daughters, Evaline (eleven years old) and Eldora (nine years old), testified that they saw Belle Gunness on July 9, several months after the fire. The *Bee* reported their testimonies.

> Hutson, a neighbor of Mrs. Gunness and one of the men engaged by Sheriff Smutzer to dig in the ruins for the bodies at the time of the fire, declared he knew Mrs. Gunness so well that he could not be mistaken. He said:
>
> "I saw her on the road near the hog pen July 9. I was returning from town with a hayrick and saw two people at the Gunness place. She had on a light skirt, black waist, wide-brimmed hat, a white veil on the hat and a black veil that came to her chin.
>
> "There was a man with her. He weighed about 165 pounds and had a gray mustache and gray hair. When I got within two wagon lengths they got into the buggy and drove on and I tried to follow them. They got ahead of me and I did not like to follow them.
>
> "There was too good a chance of getting a chunk of lead. The buggy had a yellow running gear and black top. The horse was a gray one with dapples on its hips as big as a half dollar."
>
> On cross-examination the witness said he did not see the woman's features or face but could tell from her build and walk that it was Mrs. Gunness.
>
> Evaline Hutson . . . testified that she saw Mrs. Gunness in "hay time" near the woods. She was in a buggy with a man. They passed her in the road. The girl said that Mrs. Gunness had on two veils, a black one and white one, the black one being over her face. The girl said: "When I saw her, she turned her face away from me."
>
> Eldora Hutson . . . said: "I was playing by the big gate by the road. I saw Mrs. Gunness go by with a man. She had on a double veil and a wide brimmed hat. I did not know the man."

Daniel said that another neighbor, Martha Schetter, unaware he had seen Belle that day, told him she had seen Belle as well.

Decades later, when Eldora and Evaline were grown women, they still believed it was Belle they saw that day in July.

Fred Lambright, one of Belle's neighbors, also claimed to have seen Belle in July. The *Daily Republican* reported:

> Fred Lambright . . . claims that one night in July as he was driving to town, he saw a man and a woman in a buggy, drawn by a gray horse, drive into the Gunness yard. . . . According to his story, he watched

them and heard the woman say: "The money ain't here," after she had jumped out of the rig and walked around the ruins of the burned house. The woman, he alleges, was very much like Mrs. Gunness in appearance and the voice was similar to that of the alleged murderess. The man he did not recognize. He says he did not tell anybody about the matter because he was afraid of being laughed at.

When Lambright told his story to Albert, the sheriff disdainfully dismissed it, refused to take a statement, and ridiculed him, asking if Lambright was sure he had not seen a ghost since Belle was dead. At first, he was baffled by Albert's behavior, but as time went on, Lambright began to believe that the sheriff was somehow working with and protecting Belle.

Over the years, credible sightings of Belle Gunness died down. It was not until 1931 that Belle's return seemed possible when dead bodies started to pile up at the feet of another woman.

Esther Carlson, née Johnston, was a frail woman who immigrated from Sweden in 1892. At first glance, Esther had little in common with Belle. The former was younger and smaller in stature than Belle. She never lived in Indiana but instead moved out west to California and Arizona. Despite these differences, the similarity of their crimes convinced many that Esther was indeed Belle. She denied being the La Porte killer until her last breath.

Esther's first husband, whom she met out east and married in 1908, drowned just months after their marriage. During her second marriage to Charles Colson, Gustav Ahlzen came to stay with them. Gustav, a recent immigrant from Sweden, became ill, and a doctor was called to the house to examine him. Diagnosing a heart condition, the doctor prescribed strychnine tablets to be taken as needed. He was soon called back to the house to find Gustav dead from an overdose of strychnine. Whether he accidentally overdosed, died by suicide, or was murdered was an open question never to be resolved. Following in Gustav's footsteps, Esther's second husband expired after fourteen years of marriage amid suspicions he'd been poisoned. Ultimately, his death was attributed to stomach cancer—though symptoms of strychnine poisoning are very similar. Just like with Belle, there were more cadavers to come.

After the deaths of Charles and Gustav, Esther went to work as a housekeeper for August Lindstrom. After fourteen years, her employment came to an abrupt halt when August decided to move in with one of his sons.

Before she could lose her job, August died. An autopsy showed he'd ingested enough arsenic to kill forty people. Esther argued that it was just a coincidence that she'd purchased arsenic shortly before August's death and that it was just happenstance that she had made herself a co-beneficiary of his $2,000 bank account just a few days before he died.

Not long after August's death, Anna Erickson, Esther's neighbor, was taken to the hospital due to "effects of poisoning similar to that believed to have killed Lindstrom." While recovering, Anna reported to Deputy District Attorney George Stahlman, who was investigating "the alleged fatal poisoning of August Lindstrom," that "Mrs. Carlson cared for an aged man in Hemet prior to the death of Mrs. Carlson's husband in 1925. This man died."

It was later revealed that Esther and Anna had been friends and neighbors as well as coconspirators to obtain August's money. The relationship had since frayed, for obvious reasons. Anna was upset because Esther served Anna a cup of poisoned coffee, sending her to the hospital where she was not expected to survive.

August's sons, Peter and Charles, learned about the strange note giving Esther access to their father's bank account. Peter, who lived in Chicago, and Charles, who was in Williams, came to Lomita, investigated, and then notified police of their concerns. Esther's past life soon aroused suspicions. People began to question the number of men in Esther's orbit who were dropping dead: her first husband, Charles Colson, Gustav Ahlzen, the elderly man she cared for in Hemet, and August Lindstrom. Esther was sixty-two years old in 1931 when she was arrested for the murder of August Lindstrom.

Esther's body count was by no means murder on Belle's scale, but it was enough to make people question if the two women were one and the same when the Lindstrom case made national news. Adding to the mystery was the discovery of a photograph of three children, taken more than twenty years ago, that belonged to Esther. Mary Kruger identified the photograph as a picture of Belle's children.

John (Dennis) Daily and John A. Yorkey, who were both from La Porte and had known Belle, viewed Esther's body shortly after her death. After spending almost an hour with the corpse, the two

Bicycles and a car along the road to Belle's farm. *Photo courtesy of the Steve Shook Collection.*

men stated they were positive that Belle and Esther were the same woman. But this was in 1931, and they had not seen Belle since 1908, making it hard to judge the accuracy of their identification.

It would take almost eighty years before genealogical research proved that Esther was not Belle. In the end, it was just another false lead. Although Esther did kill multiple people, she was no Belle Gunness.

In 2007, attorney and forensic anthropologist Andrea Simmons led a team of graduate students from the University of Indianapolis in the exhumation of the body buried in the grave of Belle Gunness at Forest Home Cemetery. Simmons, a La Porte native who had grown up listening to horror stories about Belle Gunness, was writing her dissertation on the murderess. Under the direction of forensic anthropologist Stephen Nawrocki, Simmons oversaw the seven-hour exhumation. Their goal was to do a DNA comparison to find out whether the body was Belle's. But the sample they were able to retrieve was too insubstantial to provide a match.

Simmons hopes to reexamine the remains soon using the advanced technology now available to make a match. "If we can get the DNA, we'll be able to say whether the person in the grave is related to Belle's sister's descendants," said Simmons, noting that family members had given permission to conduct the exhumation.

16

Endings

WHEN JULIUS TRUELSON LEFT HIS NEW BRIDE, ARABELLA, IN Montreal with a bad check to cover their hotel expenses, he boarded a train to Detroit. From there, he caught the train to La Porte. He spent part of the journey talking to an attorney from Toronto named J. D. Montgomery, who Julius said would remember him getting off at La Porte and could substantiate his story. A quick internet search shows there was a practicing attorney named J. D. Montgomery in Toronto in 1908 whose law offices were located at Church and King Streets. No one appears to have contacted Mr. Montgomery to verify Julius's story.

Arriving at Belle's around 10 p.m., Julius found Ray already there with an upset Belle.

"She told me one of her victim's husband or rather brother was coming to look for him and she wanted me to fire the place and go with her to Frisco," Julius confessed later. He advised her to stand pat to avoid suspicion.

"She wanted Lamphere and I to stay all night, but we thought it best to go to town. Lamphere and I decided that we had to put her out of the way before she did us up, so we tossed a coin to see which of us was to do the job. Lamphere lost, and it was decided that he was to enter at night and knock Belle and her kids in the head and set fire to the place to cover her crimes and ours."

Julius said he left La Porte shortly after that, ending up in Texas, where he was arrested. In 1910, he was still in prison.

Ray Lamphere with a pretty bouquet of flowers in the background.
Photo courtesy of the La Porte County Historical Society.

After that, he faded from history. A Julius G. Truelson became a noted educator in Texas, and the dates match. He certainly had the brains and capabilities. But no one knows for sure if this was Belle's Julius.

Albert Smutzer was voted out of office in 1908, having served one term. In the past, he'd worked as a funeral director and owned a tavern, which remains in the Smutzer family to this day. It was rumored that he moved to Texas and bought a grapefruit farm after his time as sheriff. Though it sounds lovely, there is no collaborative evidence or contemporary newspapers citing that he ended his days walking through acres of fragrant grapefruit orchards.

The rest of Albert's story is found in fragments, gleaned from news accounts, books, and contemporary records. At first, his life seemed grand. Albert remained in La Porte, and the local Republican party considered nominating him for state representative. He seemed to have plenty of money for investing in business ventures because that same year an article in *Motor Age* stated that the ex-sheriff was running an agency selling vehicles for two Indianapolis companies—Overland Automobiles and the National Motor Vehicle. Around the same time, other articles reported that Albert, in a partnership with G. H. Greiger, would soon be opening a large garage in La Porte.

A year later, according to the *South Bend Tribune*, Albert left for an extended trip through northern and central Indiana, visiting cities such as Kokomo, Lafayette, and Indianapolis, to demonstrate a newly developed emergency automobile tire. When Albert returned home, a factory manufacturing these emergency tires opened and was expected to employ around twenty men.

His life remained uneventful until 1913, when bold headlines informed readers that Albert had been charged by the state for stealing approximately $3,000 in fees during his time as sheriff.

The next year was no better. On March 9, 1914, the *Joliet Evening Herald-News* reported Albert had been missing for two weeks. The paper referred to a shooting in Michigan City that left Albert injured before he disappeared. The article does not explain how or why he was shot. Upon his return, Albert surrendered to the police on a charge of passing a bad check. Two of his La Porte friends bailed him out, and he returned home.

Albert surfaced again in 1932 when he was up for the Republican nomination to represent Porter and La Porte Counties but was unsuccessful. Two years later, he gave an interview to two reporters from the *Herald Argus*. "There were a lot of ridiculous rumors that have cropped up about my leaving but that was only newspaper talk," said Albert. He claims he had been traveling around the country working construction in Chicago, Fort Worth, and Tucson. At the time, according to Sylvia Shepherd, a former reporter and editor for the *Chicago Tribune*, who wrote *The Mistress of Murder Hill*, Albert was living in the home of his daughter, where he would remain until his death seven years later on October 2, 1940.

Ray did well in prison. He followed directions, did his chores as required, and seemed to adjust well to his new living situation. But within the year, he was diagnosed with a rapidly spreading form of tuberculosis. During his last months, he grew close to a fellow convict named Harry Myers, who became a loyal and faithful friend. Harry, who didn't know much about the Gunness case as prisoners received newspapers stripped of crime news, became Ray's confidant and in the process learned a lot about the murders.

Ray told Harry that Belle had paid him $500 to help her get away. Several days before the fire, Belle was in Chicago and saw a woman sitting on a flight of stairs crying. Belle offered her a job and a place to stay at the farm. She thought the woman would be a good enough substitute for her own body.

There were a few difficulties; the woman had a full set of teeth, long beautiful hair, and the shape of her nose differed from Belle's. This necessitated the decapitation, and Belle had Ray make a box for the head, which he then buried somewhere near the orchard.

After killing her three children and placing them in the cellar, Belle took a few extra moments to tuck Philip's young body under the protective arm of the woman and then met Ray, who was waiting for her with a horse and buggy. In Belle's possession were satchels filled with money totaling about $30,000 as well as jewelry and other valuables. Ray drove her to a prearranged rendezvous point, where another accomplice waited. Ray claimed not to know who the man was, but he did know their destination: Chicago.

Ray returned to the house, started the fire, and then walked to the Wheatbrooks' farm. The plan was for Belle, once she was safe, to send Ray her false teeth to place in the cellar.

Parts of Ray's story coincide with other witnesses' testimony. Two neighbors on the night of the fire saw Belle riding in a buggy. It also matched Julius's statement that Belle wanted to burn down her house and flee.

Ray was pathetically in love with this cold-blooded murderess. It didn't matter that she probably would have murdered him just as she had all the others. Ray once said he'd overheard Belle and Helgelien discussing how best to poison him and felt Belle's rage when he wouldn't take out an insurance policy on himself naming her as a beneficiary. But none of this was a deal breaker for Ray.

Belle, he told Harry, was living in Chicago disguised as a man. Later he told Harry that Belle was living near La Porte. Ray had a cache of letters and cards delivered to him in prison that he said contained information about Belle under her code name of Big Six. He didn't allow Harry to read them though.

He also talked about how Belle dispatched her victims by putting chloral hydrate or strychnine in their coffee and, as they lay dying, clobbering them over the head. Sometimes she crept into their rooms and beat them to death with a club.

There were aspects of dark humor in some of his tales. Ray recalled digging a grave for one victim when a man destined to become the next showed up early, throwing the tight schedule of murders and burials out of sync. There was an episode where Ray decided to use a bachelor neighbor's land as a burial spot since the neighbor and Belle had been feuding. Unfortunately, as he stepped down from the buggy, the horse took off along with the corpse. Then there was the night he had hurried to bury three bodies.

As the tuberculosis wreaked havoc on his body, Ray confided in Harry that some of Belle's fortune remained hidden away on her property, including a box filled with diamonds. Also remaining was a buried box holding the head of the decapitated corpse. With Ray's permission, Harry contacted Wirt, telling him about the head though leaving out the diamonds. Wirt and several men went to the spot Ray had described but despite hours of digging didn't find anything. They sent back for clearer instructions, received them, and then still failed to find the head. Finally there were no more directions. Ray had passed away.

Roy Johnson, who produced, with filmmaker Stephen Ruminski, *The Gunness Mystery*, used the profits from their documentary to buy gravestones for those of Belle's victims buried in unmarked graves. That included Ray Lamphere, whom Johnson believed was also one of her victims.

Harry served another year in prison and was about to be released and paroled under Wirt and Weir's custody when he received a

A grisly scene showing four decayed bodies removed from a hole in the ground on the Gunness farm. *Photo courtesy of the Steve Shook Collection.*

letter signed by Charley Hunter, stating, "She has moved." The writer also offered Harry a job. Not knowing a Charley Hunter, Harry didn't reply. Sometime later, when he was living in La Porte, another letter arrived. In this missive, the writer acknowledged that Hunter wasn't his real name but that he was a relative of the accused accomplice. Harry ignored this one as well.

For a while, Harry looked for the diamonds—and possibly the head. Then one day he just wasn't there anymore. He might have grown tired of searching and decided to move on. He was a drifter, after all. Or perhaps he found the diamonds and packed up and headed out of town. Of course, there's a third scenario. Big Six, Charley Hunter, and the gang had him under surveillance, and when he unearthed the gems, they killed him and took the stones with them. Whatever took place, no one heard from Harry again.

What really happened that night? Let's consider the possibilities.

There's a photo of Ray in jail, his face gaunt, his eyes wide with his typical deer-caught-in-the-headlights look. Behind him is a large bouquet of flowers. Susie Richter, retired curator at the La Porte County Historical Society, believes that's proof that he and Belle were still in collusion and that she was alive.

"Where else would he get the flowers?" she asked. It is indeed a good question. But what if Belle was dead and whoever killed her wanted Ray to think she was still alive?

Lillian de la Torre, author of *The Truth About Belle Gunness*, believes that Ray was telling the truth when he claimed Belle was paying off Sheriff Smutzer. If the two were partners, then logic says it was Albert who was waiting for Belle the night of the fire.

"She was infatuated with her own power and her own cleverness that she did not see what she had done," writes de la Torre. "She richly deserved to die, and she had, in effect, put up $30,000 [the amount de la Torre said she was carrying] to be had without risk as a reward for murdering her. Had she signed her own death warrant?"

De la Torre says yes. Her theory was that Albert, realizing that Belle would kill him once she was safe, planned, for his own safety, to kill her first.

"It was on the cards that when she had used him, she would destroy him," writes de la Torre. "It was on the cards that he knew it. When she tried it, did she at last meet her match?"

Let's suppose that Albert was on Belle's payroll but didn't know the extent of her crimes until after the fire. He was an accomplice to a murderess and would go to jail if not to the gallows if he were found out. He agreed to help her escape and then, knowing that safety for Belle meant no witnesses, figured she was going to do him in that night. Knowing it was either him or her, he made his plans.

When would she try to kill him? Probably right before they reached their destination. So he had to be ready to move fast. He tucked his gun into his pocket or somewhere close and waited until the time was right. He didn't hesitate and shot to kill. It was close range, but still Belle likely struggled. She wasn't one to give up easily and now she was mad. But finally it was done. Albert didn't have time to lose.

He dragged her into the woods, buried her, took the money, cleaned up the blood, and drove back fast to La Porte, arriving just before Joe knocked on his door at 5 a.m. He acted sleepy, but he hadn't slept all night long. There was no time to rest. He needed to convince the world Belle died in the fire Ray set, and so he still had a lot to do.

Wirt Worden and his client Ray Lamphere in the courtroom. *Photo courtesy of the La Porte County Historical Society.*

At first it went well; everyone thought Belle died and Ray murdered her. Albert locked Ray up the same day as the fire so he couldn't get drunk at one of his favorite watering holes and babble about what really went down.

But then things started to go wrong. Wirt and his legal team weren't just going through the motions to make their money; they were hitting hard. People were speculating about the body size and the missing head. Then Coroner Mack refused to declare Belle dead. That required Albert to travel again at night, find the buried body, and dig her back up. Albert stuck his hand in her mouth and yanked, probably more than once, pulling out the bridge. Then he covered her with dirt once again.

Albert hired Klondike to "find" the bridgework, which testimony indicated had not been through such a ferocious fire. He then sent weird messages about "Big Six" to Ray, who would do anything to help the woman he loved, and, in this case, that meant keeping quiet.

Yes, Albert Smutzer could have done it. But did he? He'd never been known as a violent man, though if he had no choice, then maybe. A car just like his was seen speeding down the road leading to

Belle's; others saw his red roadster in towns west of La Porte and east of Chicago. And after the fire, Albert had money—a lot of money.

But maybe it was someone else. Belle had other associates over the years. J. S. Blackney, the owner of a matrimonial agency in St. Joseph, Michigan, that Belle used, was a possibility. Or perhaps one of the women who worked for Blackney, Ina Goodenough. Ina had been married to Milo Piper, who was a bigamist and murderer, and he had physically abused Ina. When Ina was arrested in Chicago for running another matrimonial agency under a different name, Milo Piper was there for her. Belle would have known Ina through Blackney. Would Belle have called her for help in getting away? And would Ina have then asked Milo, who we know was capable of murder, to help Belle? Could he have been the man waiting for Ray to drop her off? Sure, Ina might have asked him to help Belle, but Milo liked money, and he had been violent toward women before, so it is not a baseless theory that Milo (either with or without Ina's blessing) killed Belle and took off with the money. However, I think Belle was much smarter than Milo and would have watched for any movement that might have indicated he was going to harm her. And we know Belle knew her way around guns and sharp knives. So, although Milo could have gone rogue, he'd be the one dead not Belle. One can imagine she'd have a knife in his side before he even knew what had happened. Milo doesn't get my vote. But perhaps Belle made a call to the Levee instead.

In this scenario, when Ray and Belle arrived at the meeting spot, one of Hinky Dink and Bathhouse's enforcers was there. Was he there to take Belle back to the city, or did she know too much, have too many people on her trail? Could she bring the law down on them? He could have easily taken her out and hid the body. Maybe he did a quick calculation and decided she was worth more alive than dead. With her brains, cunning, and business acumen, she could set up shop in the Levee. Or buy another farm. Besides, Hinky Dink and Bathhouse were the law in the Levee. Ray said she was living somewhere close to La Porte.

Author Sylvia Shepherd believed Belle escaped, writing she was too smart to be killed by an accomplice. But even the smartest people can eventually run into someone capable of outwitting them.

As someone who has lived with Belle, so to speak, for the last three years, immersed in trial transcripts, autopsy reports, interviews, books, and newspaper articles, I agree with Sylvia Shepherd up to a point. Belle was too smart to die in the fire; she got away that night. But I don't believe she was infallible. Nobody is. Maybe she lived to a ripe old age, or maybe she met a fate similar to the one she dealt out. I also agree with Lillian de la Torre that Belle met up with Albert that night.

I might change my mind tomorrow; I've changed it plenty of times before. But as I'm writing this, here's what I believe. Albert wasn't violent; there's nothing in his biography to indicate he was. Of course, you can argue that anyone with their back to the wall can be dangerous. Sure, he took money from the sheriff's department and from Belle to look the other way. But that night, he did what he was supposed to: he took her to wherever they'd planned—most likely to one of the train stations on the road where his distinctive sports car was noted—and Belle gave him a lot of money to do so. She made it to Chicago and met up with denizens of the Levee who had been her partners long before she bought the farm. Why else move to America, make a fortune, wear silk dresses, live in fine houses, and then go back to hauling 150 pounds of potatoes and chasing pigs through mud unless it was at their behest? If she wanted to get away from her neighborhood, she could have moved somewhere else in the city. It was Chicago after all—there were plenty of places to go. Dressed as a man, like Ray said, Belle could have lived without fear in the Levee or really almost anywhere in Chicago. She no longer had the farm to entice men, but she would have thought of something. She was Belle.

I also believe Belle was in alliance with Hoch. Belle had a German-speaking accomplice or maybe two. German was a very common language in the Midwest back then, particularly in Indiana, Ohio, Wisconsin, and Illinois. That swath of the Midwest was known as the German belt because of the huge influx of Germans who began immigrating in droves to the United States starting in 1849. Fred Hafle's story backs this up—the man he described could well have been Hoch who spoke German.

Hoch and Belle seemed a perfect match—both plying their trade in similar manners. Between her Scandinavian roots and his German heritage, they could take advantage of a lot of lonely immigrants. Belle buried some of his victims on her farm—Tina, Mary, Clara (or Frances), Anna, Esther, and maybe more. But she didn't do it for free; she charged a fee. She was that type of woman—everything had a price. She was greedy and soulless. The ultimate psychopathological narcissist.

It was long assumed that Liz Smith knew much more about the night of the fire than she ever told. She promised Wirt that she would tell it all in the end. In 1916, she was horribly burned when her house caught on fire, and friends took her in and nursed her. She was seventy-nine years old then and very feeble and the burns were terrible. Knowing she was going to die, she sent for Wirt, but he was on a fishing trip in Louisiana and out of instant communication. By the time he could return, Liz was dead, taking her secrets about the Gunness affair with her.

Liz left a sizable estate for an African American woman—or really an average White American—in the early 1900s. According to records, Wirt was paid $500 out of her estate. Wirt gave Ray an excellent defense, yet Ray didn't have a penny to his name. When he was asked who was paying for the defense, Wirt never answered. Many suspected Liz was paying the tab, and that $500 would have gone a long way toward the top-notch defense Wirt and his team provided.

As for the valuables buried on the property, they are probably still there. Belle couldn't take it all with her and, wisely, wouldn't have. She was probably counting on Ray to bring it to her, not realizing that Albert would throw him in jail the very day of the fire. That's what compelled Belle to come back, heavily veiled, in July 1908 as seven witnesses reported. Maybe there were even more people who saw her that day and passed on the information to Albert, who discouraged them from saying any more about it.

Did Harry Myers find the fortune and disappear? I'd like to think so. He was kind to Ray when he was dying, and it would be a better ending than Belle getting her hands on it. Unfortunately, that's the least likely option. Big Six, Charley Hunter, and "a relative of the accused accomplice" seemed like the kind of guys who wouldn't let a fortune slip away. Big Six and associates certainly seemed to know where Harry was. They could have kept an eye on him and, when he uncovered the gold, grabbed the treasure, knocked him over the head, and buried his body—the farm was a graveyard after all.

Richter showed me a photo snapped near the shed from Belle's farm that was disassembled and then put back together as part of the exhibit.

"Look at this," she said, pointing to a young boy—a visitor to the museum. At his side I see the hazy outline of what looks to be a large woman.

Richter, who seems very much like a no-nonsense historian and researcher, said that those who work in the museum often feel as though Belle is with them, particularly in the area where the artifacts from her life, her farm, and her victims are on display. This makes sense. Since she burned down her farm, where else would she go?

As for Asle Helgelien, the hero of our story, he wrote a letter to his siblings in Norway dated May 21, 1908:

It is not yet known how many she murdered. It was a horrible thing to see. If there were any in her own family, she thought might discover murders, she got them to her house and finished them off.

Anders was not the first, but I believe he became the last, which they can thank me for. Anders was buried on May 5th in the cemetery or graveyard in La Porte, Indiana. He was buried in the Norwegian Lutheran Church. The funeral oration was given by August Johnsen. It was too far to take him here to Dakota; it is about 800 miles.

It is sad to think about, but one thing I am happy about is that he did not cause any of his misfortune, he was deceived into his death. Nobody would have thought a woman could be so false and that could operate this murder house for such a long time close to the city limit without the authorities finding out sooner. But she went regularly to church and everything nice and in a big way. I am satisfied that I found all which happened. He now rests in peace. It is sad, but several have suffered an untimely death and have been themselves the cause of it, and so many live their days in prisons and mental hospitals, which is worse.

I ask, brother and sister, that you do not grieve too much, it could have been worse. We are well at this date and wish the same for you. I could write much more but the letter is now going in the mail. What the final outcome will be and how many accomplices Bella Gunness has had is not yet known. They are still investigating. I will probably have to go there again.

Our younger brother is here now and helps me. I am now about finished with the spring chores.

Greetings from your brother.
Asle Knudsen Helgelien

Andrew Helgelien's gravestone, located at Patton Cemetery in La Porte. *Photo courtesy of Dale Hoppe.*

The inscription on Andrew's tombstone reads, "The Last Victim of the Gunness Horror. Remains Found by His Brother Asle K. Helgelien, May 5, 1908. Rest in Peace."

Maybe someday we'll know what really happened. For now, it's all supposition. All we can be sure of, at this date, is that Belle is finally gone, her evil interred somewhere. And let's hope there's never another like her.

BIBLIOGRAPHY

Publications

Wilbur, Cressy L., ed. *Annual Report of the Secretary of State on the Registra-tion of Births and Deaths, Marriages and Divorces in Michigan for the Year 1900.* http://www.mdch.state.mi.us/osr/annuals/archives/1901.pdf

Baumann, Edward, and John O'Brien. "Hell's Belle." *Chicago Tribune Mag-azine*, March 1987.

Chapman, Charles C. *History of La Porte County, Indiana and History of Indi-ana.* Chicago, IL: Blakely, Brown & Marsh, 1880.

de la Torre, Lillian. *The Truth About Belle Gunness.* New York: Fawcett Pub-lications, 1955.

Duke, Thomas. *Celebrated Criminal Cases of America.* San Francisco: James Barry, 1910.

Guild, Arthur Alden. *Baby Farms in Chicago: An Investigation Made for the Juvenile Protection Agency.* Chicago: The Juvenile Protection Agency, 1917.

Hearn, Daniel Allen. *Legal Executions in Illinois, Indiana, Iowa, Kentucky and Missouri: A Comprehensive Registry, 1866–1965.* Jefferson, NC: McFarland & Company, 2016.

German and Scandinavian Immigrants in the American Midwest, The Gilded Age and Progressive Era: Student Research Projects, Wash-ington State University.

Jones, Ann. *Women Who Kill.* New York: Fawcett Create, 1980.

Jordan, Rosan A., and Susan J. Kalcik, eds. *Women's Folklore, Women's Culture.* Philadelphia: University of Pennsylvania Press, 1985.

Langlois, Janet L. *Belle Gunness: The Lady Bluebeard*. Bloomington: Indiana University Press, 1985.

La Porte County Historical Society. *The Gunness Story*. La Porte, IN: author.

Larson, Erik. *The Devil in the White City: Murder, Magic, and Madness at the Fair That Changed America*. New York: Crown Publishing, 2003.

Lindberg, Richard. *Heartland Serial Killers: Belle Gunness, Johann Hoch, and Murder for Profit in Gaslight Era Chicago*. DeKalb: Northern Illinois University Press, 2011.

Newton, Michael. *Hunting Humans: An Encyclopedia of Modern Serial Killers*. Port Townsend, WA: Loompanics Unlimited, 1990.

Ramsland, Katherine. *Many Secrets, Many Graves*. Notorious USA, 2014.

Schechter, Harold. *Hell's Princess: The History of Belle Gunness, the Butcher of Men*. New York: Little A, 2018.

Schechter, Harold, ed. *True Crime: An American Anthology*. New York: Library of America, 2008.

Shepherd, Sylvia Elizabeth. *Mystery of Murder Hill: The Serial Killings of Belle Gunness*. Bloomington, IN: 1st Books Library, 2001.

Selzer, Adam. *H. H. Holmes: The True History of the White City*. New York: Skyhorse, 2017.

Wilson, Colin. *A Plague of Murder: The Rise and Rise of Serial Killing in the Modern Age*. London: Constable & Robinson Ltd., 1995.

Woolridge, Clifton Rodman. *Twenty Years a Detective in the Wickedest City in the World*. Chicago: Chicago Publishing Company, 1908.

DVDs

Only Belle: A Serial Killer from Selbu. Directed by Anne Berit Vestby. National Film Network, 2006.

The Gunness Mystery. Written by Bruce Johnson; directed by Stephen Ruminski. PC Video Productions, 2010.

Periodicals

Argos Herald

Atchison Daily Globe (Atchison, Kansas)

Baltimore Sun

Bellingham Herald (Bellingham, WA)

Belvedere Daily Republic (Belvedere, IL)

Bremen Banner (Bremen, IN)

Bremen Enquirer (Bremen, IN)

Brooklyn Daily Eagle

Chicago Tribune
Des Moines Register
The Daily Appeal (Carson City, NV)
Daily News (New York, NY)
Detroit Free Press
Elkhart Daily
Elkhart Daily Review
Elkhart Review
Elkhart Truth
Evansville Press (Evansville, IN)
Evening News (Wilkes-Barre, PA)
Fort Wayne Daily News (Fort Wayne, IN)
Fort Wayne Weekly Sentinel
Goshen Daily Democrat
Herald-Press (St. Joseph, MI)
Inter Ocean (Chicago)
Indianapolis News
Indianapolis Star
Ironton County Register (Ironton, MO)
La Porte County Herald-Argus
La Porte Herald-Argus
La Porte Weekly Herald
Logansport Pharos-Tribune
Logansport Reporter
Los Angeles Times
Marion Star (Marion, OH)
New York Evening World
New York Times
News Palladium (Benton Harbor, MI)
Oshkosh Northwestern (Oshkosh, WI)
Ottumwa Tri-Weekly Courier (Ottumwa, IA)
Palladium-Item (Richmond, IN)
Perrysburg Journal (Perrysburg, OH)
The Philadelphia Press (Pittsburgh, PA)
Pittsburgh Press
The Raleigh Times (Raleigh, NC)
Richmond Item (Richmond, IN)
Richmond Planet (Richmond, IN)
St. Louis Dispatch
The San Francisco Call
San Francisco Caller

Standard-Sentinel (Hazleton, PA)
Star-Gazette (Elmira, New York)
South Bend Tribune
Swayzee Press (Swayzee, IN)
The Tampa Tribune (Tampa, FL)
The Times (Munster, IN)
Warren Times Mirror (Warren, PA)
The Washington Post
Watertown Daily Times
Washington Herald (Washington, DC)
Wilkes-Barre Times Leader

Websites

Historical Crime Detective, http://www.historicalcrimedetective.com
Mysterious Chicago Tours, http://mysteriouschicago.com
Psychology Today, https://www.psychologytoday.com/us/blog/wicked
   -deeds/201906/the-unique-motives-female-serial-killers

Ever since she asked for a magnifying glass when she was eight so she could start looking for clues, **Jane Simon Ammeson** has loved mysteries. She's now upped her game and writes historic true crime. She is the author of 15 books, including *How to Murder Your Wealthy Lovers and Get Away With It*, *Murder & Mayhem in the Gilded Age*, *Hauntings of the Underground Railroad*, and *Murders that Made Headlines: Crimes of Indiana*. Her travel book, *Lincoln Road Trips: The Back-Roads Guide to America's Favorite President*, won the bronze in the Lowell Thomas Travel Journalism Awards.